# A SCIENTIFIC MODEL OF HISTORY

# A SCIENTIFIC MODEL OF HISTORY

Where is the Future Leading Us

JUAN J. GOMEZ-IBARRA

Writers Advantage
New York  Lincoln  Shanghai

**A Scientific Model of History**
Where is the Future Leading Us

All Rights Reserved © 2003 by Juan Jose Gomez Ibarra

No part of this book may be reproduced or transmitted in any form or by any means, graphic, electronic, or mechanical, including photocopying, recording, taping, or by any information storage retrieval system, without the written permission of the publisher.

Writers Advantage
an imprint of iUniverse, Inc.

For information address:
iUniverse
2021 Pine Lake Road, Suite 100
Lincoln, NE 68512
www.iuniverse.com

ISBN: 0-595-26108-6

Printed in the United States of America

*To my parents,
Juan and Mercedes*

# CONTENTS

INTRODUCTION .................................................................................xi

### PART ONE:
### FOUR VARIABLES: NATURAL RESOURCES, POPULATION, TECHNOLOGY AND STANDARD OF LIVING AND WHY THEY ARE INEXTRICABLY LINKED

1. POPULATION .........................................................................3
   Malthus' Principle—Influence of Malthus' Thinking on Darwin's and Wallace's Theory of Natural Selection—Fixed Relationship Between Natural Populations and Nature's Scarcity or Abundance

2. TECHNOLOGY .......................................................................9
   Human Ability to Thrive Indefinitely in Population Numbers—Definition of Technology Unconscious Development of Technology—The Goal of Technology

3. STANDARD OF LIVING ......................................................14

## PART TWO:
## THE HISTORY OF THE PAST

4. AN HYPOTETICAL PREHISTORIC SCENARIO ................19
   Random Differentiation—Arising of New Ways of Life—Extinction of the Original Ways of Life—Technological Transference—Demographic-Technologic Cycles

5. TOYNBEE'S MODEL OF HISTORY .......................................26
   Toynbee's Twenty-One Civilizations—Toynbee's Four Phases—Challenge-and-Response Principle—Opposed Demographical Behaviors

6. WAR ................................................................................35
   Early Stabilization—The Effects of War Pressures on Technological Development—The Nature of War

7. THE ANCIENT EGYPT, AN EXTINCT SOCIETY ..............45
   The Added Effects of Competition—History as a Shared Experience

8. ADVANCED SOCIETIES AND LESS-ADVANCED ONES ....50
   The Demographic Weakness of Developed Nations—Popular Explanations for Opposed Demographic Behaviors—Universal Mechanisms Checking Population Growth—Stabilization within Primitive Groups—Malthus' Preventive Check—Depopulation within Developed Societies—A Global Demographic Model—The Technologic-Demographic Transference Effect—The "Threat" of Less-Developed Nations

9. TODAY'S MOST POPULATED COUNTRIES .......................68
   The Reasons Behind the Apparent Backwardness of China and India—Demographic Explosions in Historic Times—China and India's Imminent Transformation

## PART THREE:
## THE HISTORY OF THE FUTURE

10. THE TECHNOLOGY OF THE FUTURE ...............................87
    Feynman's Talk—Drexler's Approach—Dangers of a Molecular Technology

11. APPROACHING THE NATURAL LIMITS ..........................92
    A Limit Technology—Inexhaustible Natural Resources—A Fixed Standard of Living—Social Limitations and other Objections

12. THE LIMITS OF THE ECONOMIC SYSTEM ......................97
    Fixed Social Structure—Normal Distribution of Aptitudes—Unequal Distribution of Income—Individual Differences as the Cause of Social Stratification—Creative Minorities—Social Selection Mechanisms—Limits of Redistribution Mechanisms

13. THE LIMITS OF CIVILIZATION .........................................108
    Civilized Behaviors—Individual Failures Coming from the Average Sector—Uncivilized Behaviors

14. MARX'S FORGOTTEN CONTRIBUTION .........................116
    Universal Social Forces—Struggle of Classes—Self-correcting Nature of Class Struggles

15. THE FEMALE OF THE SPECIES ........................................123
    Unequal Social Importance of the Sexes—Sexual Dominance in Nature—Pair-Formation in Monogamous Species—Mating in Solitary Species

16. THE END OF GROWTH .....................................................133
   Worldwide Decrease of Fertility Rates—Towards an All-Developed World—Substitution of Competence by Cooperation—Multinational States

17. THE POST-CIVILIZED WORLD .........................................140
   Civilization as an Evolutionary System—Conditions for Stabilization—Need for a Near-perfect Social Organization—Biological Homogenization—Gender Equality Regained—The Last Stage of Technological Evolution—Technology Versus Science

BIBLIOGRAPHY ...............................................................................157
NOTES AND REFERENCES ...........................................................159
ABOUT THE AUTHOR ...................................................................161

# INTRODUCTION

The idea that history cannot be treated as a scientific subject is groundless. Though the fact that no known scientific theory of history has been yet developed is no proof of the unfeasibility of such an analysis, it does provide us with the strongest argument to believe so. Thus, as the best way to prove a scientific approach to the issue of history is feasible, is to produce it, this is precisely what we will do here.

How do we intend to proceed?

All we will do is to apply the known methods to the unsolved questions.

What sort of questions are we dealing with?

How about this one: Why do civilizations decay?

The idea of civilizations decaying has been around for centuries. In the 18th century, an Englishman, Edward Gibbon, published between 1776 and 1778 a lengthy work of four volumes dealing with *"The History of the Decline and Fall of the Roman Empire."* After him, the German philosopher Oswald Spengler published between 1918 and 1922 a less lengthy, but still large work, *"The Decline of the West,"* in which he attempted to analyze history in terms of what he viewed as human "cultures" undergoing a cycle similar to that of a living organism. Later on, between 1934 and 1961, another Englishman, the history professor Arnold Joseph Toynbee, in his work, *"A Study of History,"* the most monumental endeavor of its kind, encompassing 10 volumes, tried to explain the process of human history by means of four phases that all civilizations went through, namely, those of their genesis, growth, breakdown and disintegration. What is wrong with these works? Did they not answer their issues properly? The problem is, as anyone who knows about these efforts, that these intellectuals' lengthy analysis, covering a good deal of detail, involve very complex (and thus unlikely) hypothesis.

Is there another historical question as important as the previous one?

Besides declining civilizations, the phenomena of advanced nations coexisting side by side with others much lesser-developed, appears to be constant condition throughout history. Still another Englishman, the philosopher Herbert Spencer, a contemporary of Darwin who devised his own evolutionary theories ahead of him, covering the inorganic, organic, social and cultural realms, coined the widely used phrase "survival of the fittest," only that he meant it for humans. After Darwin's own evolutionary theory was released, Spencer extended it to our species, proposing that human progress came from the triumph of the most successful societies over their inferior counterparts. Since many intellectuals soon followed Spencer's "Social Darwinism," it is no wonder that racist thinking spread widely on the late 19th and early 20th centuries. There are, however, several historical phenomena incompatible with Spencer's views, the first of them, being the very issue of decaying civilizations. Should we think of one human race as the most fit, no weakening of their societies' power should ever be perceptible, and yet, the direct descendants of the Roman founders of Londinium (today's London), hold an empire no more. Spencer's proposal is also incapable of explaining differences in development observable within countries populated either by the same race or by closely related ones, as well as regional differences within the same country. Yet another phenomenon, the extinction of formerly advanced societies, is inconsistent too with Spencer's views. The ancient Egypt represented civilization at its peak for much longer than any other historical society, and yet, vanished for good from the face of the Earth.

In the same fashion, war is another historical subject widely addressed in history books. War has prompted many intellectuals to ask themselves why is it that the human species has to fight to death among itself. Einstein and Freud exchanged letters on the subject, and interpretations of the phenomenon are as varied as an (inexplicable) atrocity flawing the human race, an undesirable collateral effect of progress, or the legitimate means of protecting a state's interests.

As many as the questions regarding historical processes might be, perhaps the most important for many has to do with its apparent chaotic nature. In past as well as recent times, prosperous eras fueled the belief that progress would eventually bring higher living standards and peace to the whole of humankind. But this sentiment was always shattered by later events. The brighter future the technological means created by the Industrial Revolution seemed to promise was darkened by the outbreak of the First World War. For many decades, the era that followed the even more destructive Second World War was not of a true peace, but that of a continued "cold" war. Therefore, skeptics doubt that future times will improve, as well as the idea of history itself having any structure. They believe it will lead us nowhere, pointing at such facts as the abyss separating the few contemporary developed nations from those in which billions of people live in permanent poverty, to credit their views.

We said that we would apply the known methods to the old questions, so we have provided a few examples of historical subjects susceptible of research. Now we need to address the issue of the method. The method we will be using is the commonly referred to as the "scientific method." Before actually trying to describe this method, I will explain how is it that I stumbled with it.

I first noticed this particular method, as it was extremely successful in destroying virtually all of my preconceptions about the world. As a kid, I strongly believed the Earth was flat, heavy objects fell faster than lighter ones, and the space surrounding us was void. When I learned the

Earth's shape was spherical, heavy objects fell at the exact same rate as lighter ones, and air filled all the space around us, these revelations came with a shock, so that I instantly developed strong objections. For instance, if the Earth was a solid sphere, how come the people living on the Southern Hemisphere did not fall downwards? I was then introduced to the notion of gravity, an invisible force dragging all objects towards the center of the Earth. But this only added to more confusion. If true, then why did not the Moon fall on the Earth? Centrifugal force, I was informed, kept the Moon orbiting our planet. At such a point, I came to suspect that this newest notion, and probably all the previous ones as well, were but smart contrivances, as centrifugal force or the friction responsible for making lighter objects to actually fall slower than heavier ones, were neither obvious nor clear to my understanding.

As I was bold enough to keep researching on this kind of subjects, I eventually found, to my astonishment, that the Moon is actually falling into the Earth, though at such a slow rate we are incapable of noticing. Much more shocking than the previous, was the revelation that space is curved. According to Einstein's theory of Relativity, the space takes the same shape of the body it surrounds. Being most solid objects in our universe roughly spherical, it turns out that space itself "curves" around them, a proposition that has been shown to fit the observations, as light beams are "bent" by big, massive objects such as stars.

As a result of this long learning process, I concluded two things. First, that the world I lived in was incredibly more complex than I could first imagine. The second thing I resolved was that the great majority of practical questions could be answered—though in the most unexpected ways—by science. Because as a student never did I find any apparent logical structure in history, and no book ever answered the many historical questions I raised when I was a child (which are the main subject of this book), I kept thinking upon them.

How could I benefit from the scientific method in order to quench my curiosity, was an issue that baffled me for a long time. I will just say that it was many years after I saw a National Geographic magazine's cover showing side by side the pictures of an astronaut donned in outer space gear, and a Guinean hunter-gatherer with his nose pierced by a bone. The magazine cover prompted me to ask myself why was it that one had evolved while the other had not. This especially annoying issue led me to read Darwin's "*On the Origin of Species,*" as its subject was evolution. Though Darwin's principle of *"Divergence of Character"* explains precisely how is it that two species sharing a common ancestor can differentiate indefinitely, I found (very much to my disappointment), that such a principle was valid only for biological evolution, and not for human societies developing technology in sharply different degrees. This was nevertheless, my starting point, and it is after two decades of work (and two more of mere guessing) that I can present my general conclusions, thanks to the scientific method.

As long as I am concerned, the scientific method is an astonishingly simple set of rules for reasoning, applicable only to natural phenomena. One accepted view of such a method[1], states that, for gaining scientific knowledge, we have to select a phenomenon, or a series of related phenomena. These phenomena are never the real, untouched phenomena as we see them occur in nature, but rather, abstract models of them. Because no natural phenomenon reproduces itself in the exact same manner (for example, a lightning's shape), we have to discard all of its aspects we regard as non-relevant. What we keep of the selected phenomena are then, abstractions referring to the regularities that identify them through time. Then we seek for invariable relationships. If we select only one phenomenon, we would need to define certain invariable aspects regarding it, and then establish an equally invariable relationship between the defined aspects. (Oddly enough, these invariable aspects are commonly known as the "variables" of a given problem; they probably got this name after their modifiable values, and not because of their changing nature.) Once we have found, for a given phenomenon, a set of variables and their fixed relationship, we try to see if the same set of variables appears in other related phenomena. Finally, if succeeding, we then proceed to construct relationships between the different phenomena, in terms of their common set of variables.

Now, here is an example of what we will do.

As mentioned, one phenomenon that has reappeared regularly throughout all of our recorded history, is war. No matter what era we select, we will find that wars have always marked the history of all known historic societies. In the same way, wars often provide the inflection point that shows if a given society is gaining a power status over others, or losing it to them. Furthermore, while considering the nature of war, we might suspect wars are related to the known trend of human populations to increase. In fact, we could choose to define war as the violent clashing of populations, belonging either to two or more different societies, or to two or more different groups within the same society (as in civil wars). We could still go on, adding the observation that wars often lead to the production of technological breakthroughs, so that a relationship between them may be inferred.

Does all of the previous mean we will attempt to construct natural laws governing war, population growth, national power and technology development?; what will these proposed "laws" will look like, equations such as $E=mc^2$?

The answers to these questions are, respectively, yes and no. If no historical laws can be found or stated even in a simple, crude form, then this whole exercise would be pointless. Laws, principles, hypothesis or statements binding the occurrence of event A with event B, and vice versa, will indeed be presented. Even when succeeding in showing some of these events (or their chosen aspects are inextricably related, no laws here will emerge under sophisticated mathematical formulas.

Equations are possible and, thus, necessary, in some fields of the scientific knowledge, notably, in physics. For example, most of what we know about physiology (how a certain hormone will determine growth), linguistics (well-defined speech structures that allow us to distinctly refer to past, present and future), or genetics (how a mutation on a single gene will produce a known disorder), etc., cannot be approached directly in a mathematical way. Even chemistry, a field closely related to physics, has developed its own set of non-mathematical formulas. Therefore, in most cases, mathematical equations are not possible in fields where nonetheless, scientific knowledge thrives. While all of the previous is true, we will be using one very simple mathematical relationship that will act as a permanent guide assisting our reasoning.

In order to start our analysis, we just need to select a given phenomenon. As stated before, most times we will not refer to a phenomenon as we see it happen in nature, but we will rather define it. So we can define, for example, the known trend of human populations to increase, as a phenomenon reappearing throughout history. While examining this phenomenon we will find its regularity a questionable one, as in these days there are human populations that tend to be stationary, and others showing a rate of negative increase. So, by the end of these lines, we will have considered these two other behaviors as well, establishing whether they also reappear in a regular way, and if so, their possible relation with other known events or phenomena.

# PART ONE

## FOUR VARIABLES: NATURAL RESOURCES, POPULATION, TECHNOLOGY AND STANDARD OF LIVING

### And Why They Are Inextricably Linked

# 1
# POPULATION

## Malthus' Principle

When researching the issue of population, English economist Thomas Robert Malthus inevitably comes up. It was Malthus who, in 1798, published a landmark work, *"An Essay on the Principle of Population."* Simply put, Malthus' principle states that population, when unchecked, increases in a geometrical ratio, while the means of subsistence increase only in an arithmetical ratio, and the consequence of the imbalance between these two forces among humans, were misery and vice.

The second premise involved in this principle—the one stating the arithmetical ratio of growth of the means of subsistence—did not, however, fit well later observations. According to the United Nations[2] humanity reached the one billion mark in 1804. For this mark to double, it took an astonishingly short period of 123 years more, that is, in 1927. Further one billion additions were achieved even faster.

We became 3 billion in 1960, that is, 33 years later; 4 billion by 1974, that is, 14 years later (thus, to double the 2 billion mark, it took only 47 years); 5 billion in 1987, that is, 13 years later; and 6 billion in 1999, that is, 12 years later (thus, to double the 3 billion mark, it now took a mere 25 years). Should we continue to grow at this rate, we would indeed, as most futurists say, have to terraform Mars, invade suitable moons within the Solar System, or expand beneath its frontiers.

But according to the United Nations projections, further one billion additions will now take longer. It will take 14 years (2013) to reach the 7 billion mark, meanwhile 15 years (2028) will pass before Earth hits the 8 billion mark, and 26 years (2054) later the planet should have 9 billion living humans. This means the rate of increase has slowed. In fact, the United Nations have estimated one day our population might stabilize; in 1988 their forecast, according to their medium-fertility scenario, was world population stabilizing at 11 billion by the year 2200[3].

Why is that our population has grown so fast in recent years? Why is the rate of increase slowing? Due to what circumstances will it probably stabilize? Since any of these questions is too complex to directly try to solve them, we will target instead, the most elemental form these questions can assume: Why is it that our population has grown at all?

## Influence of Malthus' Thinking on Darwin and Wallace's Theory of Natural Selection

While Malthus' principle did not succeed in forecasting our fast demographic growth, it proved to be most useful in other grounds. Except for those who are familiar with the subject of evolution, few people know it was Malthus' proposition that inspired two of his countrymen to draw totally unexpected and widely accepted conclusions (among scientists). It was in 1831 that Charles Robert Darwin stepped on board of H.M.S. Beagle. When he returned to England, in 1836, he did so deeply impressed by the "variability" of the life forms he had the chance to see in tropical areas. Instead of remaining as fixed forms, Darwin then knew living organisms had a tendency to change, so, on July 1837 he opened his first notebook on *"Transmutation of Species."*[4]

With his mind clearly set on the problem of variability, Darwin read Malthus' work in 18zures, 3) only the individuals that (by random chance) possess the best features to survive, pass their traits on to the next generations. This is his *"Natural Selection"* principle, featured in the complete name of his most famous work: *"On The Origin of Species by means of Natural Selection, or the Preservation of Favoured Races in the Struggle for Life,"* published in 1859.

Herbert Spencer's "survival of the fittest" expression was in turn embraced by Darwin, so that the name of the fourth chapter of Darwin's *"Origin"* is *"Natural Selection; or the Survival of the Fittest."* Why did Darwin publish his work so many years (21) after reading Malthus? There are indications that Darwin may not intended to release his major theory while still alive. Though he instructed his wife in a 1844 letter to devote 400 pounds to the publication of a sketch of his "species theory" in the case of his sudden death, Darwin later showed no hurry to publish. As it seems, he was well aware of, and feared the fierce criticism his work would unleash, and did not want to be upset by it. But fate, so to speak, had decided otherwise. Darwin was prompted to publish due to a manuscript he received in 1858 by an unknown English naturalist, Alfred Russell Wallace. The mail contained Wallace's own theory of natural selection.

As early as 1842 (17 years before publishing), Darwin had written some 35 page-long pencil notes containing his views, and these he enlarged, two years later, into his 1844 230-page long ink sketch. What Darwin found in Wallace's manuscript, were the same ideas of his 1842 pencil notes.

Under these dire circumstances, what was to be done? A nasty dispute over the primacy on the development of calculus had embittered the relationships between English physicist Isaac Newton, and his German philosopher and mathematician friend, Gottfried Wilhelm Leibniz. Leibniz developed his ideas around 1675, and published them in 1684; Newton invented his method in 1666 (11 years ahead of

Leibniz), but published—again, due of fear of criticism—in 1687 (3 years after Leibniz).

To prevent a disaster like that repeating itself, two friends of Darwin, the noted geologist Charles Lyell and Joseph Dalton Hooker, made provisions for a joint reading of the work of the two naturalists before the Linnaean Society, on July 1, 1858. The work presented on Wallace's behalf, the manuscript he sent to Darwin, bore the title *"On the Tendency of Varieties to Depart Indefinitely from the Original Type."*[5] Incredibly enough, Wallace later admitted being the work of Robert Malthus (the *"Essay"*), as the source of inspiration for his own theories.

## Fixed Relationship between Natural Populations and Nature's Scarcity or Abundance

Now, if one were a mathematician, what could one make out of the use the biologists' found for Malthus' ideas? One could propose that there is a fixed amount of life nature can sustain, by writing:

$$P=K$$

This means natural populations, represented by $P$, remain constant, unchanged through time. But such a statement would be a short-lived one. Any other mathematician, biologist, or high-school student, could point out that the amount of natural life keeps fluctuating, sometimes, even in fairly predictable ways.

Darwin himself noted this in his *"Origin."* He described how the winter of 1854-5 destroyed four fifths of the population of the birds on his own estate (he figured this by counting the number of nests). Natural life is then routinely destroyed by harsh conditions or events such as extreme weather, droughts, floods, etc., and then later restored. Such adverse conditions will either kill the populations directly, or produce the same effect by diminishing the quantity of their food sources, dwelling places, etc. Conversely, Darwin noted that when natural populations thrived well over their average numbers, epidemics appeared and decimated them.

So, one should better say that natural populations are neither fixed nor constant, but rather, constrained within certain limits. The nature of the limiting factor could be expressed as the sum of all conditions, favorable and adverse, that affect natural life. By rewriting the previous expression it this way,

$$\frac{P}{N} = K$$

we would state that natural populations, represented by $P$, bear a fixed proportion to the sum of all natural conditions, represented by $N$. A mathematician would also say that the $N$ in this expression, is the independent variable, with the value of $P$ only adjusting to it. That is, should $N$ raise its value, an increase of $P$ would follow, and vice versa; should the value of $N$ decrease, $P$ could only shrink proportionally, thus keeping the value of the expression a constant one (which is what letter $K$ stands for).

This resembles a lot Malthus' assertion contained in his "*Essay*," in the sense that "*population constantly bears a regular proportion to the food that the earth is made to produce,*"[6] though we should note that this law is valid only for natural populations, and not for human ones.

Malthus principle is an excellent example of how a flawed assumption can lead to unforeseeable solid arguments. In fact, his principle has been deemed wrong not only because it failed in its predictions. There are many known efforts to show its inconsistency in terms of its own premises. For example, one of these arguments simply states that if food availability increases according to a limited, arithmetical pattern, human populations, no matter what their tendency might be, will just have to follow the same limited pattern. But, if Malthus' principle was totally worthless, how come both Darwin and Wallace claimed it as their source of inspiration? Is there a "hidden element of truth" one should consider? This is a tough question, for "truth" is an elusive concept (at least by scientific standards). Let us see an example.

Newton's gravitation theory, one of the greatest scientific achievements of all times, was later entirely reformed by Einstein. Newton was aware of at least one flaw in his theory, as he felt very disappointed at fact that he could not provide any cause for gravity; Einstein showed the "cause" being the curved nature of space. Newton accepted centrifugal force was not related to gravity; Einstein's curved space has no need to introduce centrifugal forces. Under Newton's mechanics, two different concepts of mass were allowed; gravitational mass, and inertial mass (calculations showed both being always the same); and Einstein simply explained why they were the same.

Now, what was the "element of truth" in Newton's gravitational theory? According to what we have just said, there was none (this, for a theory still widely used today, except under the most extreme of physical circumstances, such as with black holes). Conversely, Malthus' principle has been flawed all the time, but if we could fix the contradictions between its terms (or show they only appear to be contradictory), with the resulting proposals fitting well the observations, then we would have indeed a working set of population principles.

# 2
# TECHNOLOGY

## Human Ability to Thrive Indefinitely in Population Numbers

It is clear by now that a form of Malthus' principle applies to all species, as they maintain their numbers in constant equilibrium in respect to the conditions of the environment, except for us. But why? By origin, we are part of nature, so we should assimilate in behavior to this basic pattern. Evidently, however, there must be an exclusive human feature that allows us, unlike the rest of the natural life, to steadily grow in numbers. What is this feature?

An answer to this question came to me while reading on the subject of prehistory. Some English specialists once figured England having in prehistoric times, about 5000 inhabitants, all of them hunter-gatherers. Now, this is an interesting figure probably meaning nothing, unless one tries to connect it with today's estimated of 60 million inhabitants for the same area. Rounding the current estimate to 50 million, a ratio of 1:10,000 between now and a certain prehistoric time, emerges.

How is it possible to make any territory produce 10,000 times (or $10^4$) its normal output? Malthus guess was this: *"The reason that the greater part of Europe is more populous now than it was in former times, is that the industry of the inhabitants has made these countries produce a greater quantity of human subsistence."*[7] Now, if by "industry" Malthus meant hard work, it is obvious that hard work alone cannot account for such amazing results. Anyone who has tried to increase the efficiency of anything, say, the family budget, by a meager 10 percent, will understand how big a proportion of $10^4$ is.

While trying to get a more likely answer, the term "technology" popped up in my mind. I figured that in order to make nature overproduce by a factor of $10^4$, there was no other way than to put technological devices or procedures to work. So I accepted this view.

When looking up definitions of "technology" in dictionaries, most of the time we will get such statements as "applied science," or "the application of science to commerce or industry," etc. So, by these definitions, the scientific nature of technology is clearly stressed. But according to an accepted view, the scientific method is rather new, it dates back to Galileo (1564-1642). By that time, a wealth of different cleverly devised techniques and machinery was already in use. What should we call them, pre-scientific techniques?

## Definition of Technology

In the interest of simplicity, the term "technology" will be generally applied here to "all means used by man to modify nature for his advantage or purposes." (It is not precisely "advantageous" to destroy millions of human lives using atomic bombs, but nevertheless, this is the sole purpose of such a technology.) This definition induces a change in the usual meaning of "nature." When seen through technological eyes, nature is no longer the untouched wildlife that comes with the vast extensions of land, water and sky surrounding us, but rather, it gets turned into "natural resources." By introducing in our mathematical expression the role of technology as the only factor allowing human populations to increase, we would have to write:

$$\frac{P}{NrT} = K$$

This means that the quantity of human population in one territory cannot be solely expressed as a function of the natural resources contained in it, represented by $Nr$, but also in terms of the power of the technology used by that population.

This new proposition will also prove be a short-lived one, because it still indicates that human populations remain constant. Leaving this inconsistency aside, there is still another important implication in our use of the term "technology." Abiding by our definition, we will have to accept that the cow, the horse or the dog, are all technological products. The reason behind this strange proposition is that cows, horses and dogs are never found in nature, as we now know them. The early ancestors of these animal forms are strikingly different, and in comparison, wretched. In fact, in the absence of man, all the species we know as domesticated would not exist. The following lines belong to Darwin's *"Origin"*:

> "One of the most remarkable features in our domesticated races is that we see in them adaptation, not indeed to the animal's or plant's own good, but to man's use or fancy…when we compare the dray-horse and race-horse…, the various breeds of sheep fitted either for cultivated land or mountain pasture, with the wool of one breed good for one purpose, and that of another breed for another purpose; when we compare the many breeds of dogs, each good for man in different

ways…; when we compare the host of agricultural, culinary, orchard, and flower-garden races of plants, most useful to man at different seasons and for different purposes, or so beautiful in his eyes, we must, I think, look further than to mere variability. We cannot suppose that all the breeds were suddenly produced as perfect and as useful as we now see them; indeed, in many cases, we know that this has not been their history. The key is man's power of accumulative selection: Nature gives successive variations; man adds them up in certain directions useful to him. In this sense he may be said to have made for himself useful breeds."[8]

This is in essence, Darwin's *"Selection by Man"* principle, and he leaves us no doubt about its unconscious operation:

"…for our purpose, a form of selection, which may be called unconscious, and which results from every one trying to possess and breed from the best individual animals, is more important… The pear, though cultivated in classical times, appears, from Pliny's description, to have been a fruit of very inferior quality. I have seen great surprise expressed in horticultural works at the wonderful skill of gardeners in having produced such splendid results from such poor materials; but the art has been simple, and, as far as the final result is concerned, has been followed almost unconsciously. It has consisted in always cultivating the best known variety, sowing its seeds, and, when a slightly better variety chanced to appear, selecting it, and so onwards."[9]

# Unconscious Development of Technology— The Goal of Technology

By these views, man has been producing technology, which modifies nature to his advantage, since ancient times, even without being aware of it. Agriculture might have been first developed in this way, also. Thus, the mechanism allowing technological development is apparently a very simple one.

The permanent contact with natural phenomena (or in more recent times, their careful observation) provides us with hints on how they operate. Having noticed certain features of interest, one tries to isolate and reproduce them so as to obtain a desired effect. Should one try to devise a working procedure or device and fail, one just keeps trying until success is achieved, this is, by the so-called "trial- and-error" method. Further improvements will result in an increased degree of accumulation of the desired features, with a lesser presence of the undesired ones.

Whether the knowledge involved in this process is gained in a scientific or unscientific way, is irrelevant as pertaining to the goal of technology, which we have already identified with the achievement of certain desired effects.

# 3

# STANDARD OF LIVING

The standard of life enjoyed by the nearly 60 million Britons now inhabiting their island, is enormously superior to that of the 5000 hunter-gatherers once populating the same territory. Just how big is the difference? Let us imagine a prehistoric cave dweller as popularly depicted. He would own no furnishings, wear some animal's fur for all clothing, go barefoot or clad in some rude sandals, and be sitting on the floor of his cave in front of a languid fire, devouring the remnants of his last prey. Let us translate now his standard of living into a common unit for such purposes, such as say, dollars or euros. We will assume his daily income as the lowest practical unit of a dollar or euro, which is one cent of either. (Studies carried out by international organizations such as the World Bank, show that, in these times, millions of people live on slightly more than 50 cents of a dollar a day, mostly on rural areas of the less-developed nations[10].)

By setting the daily income of the caveman in one cent, his yearly income would be $3.65. Should we raise this figure tenfold ($10^1$), he would be making $36.50 a year. When multiplying the original figure by $10^2$ we would get $365.00, at $10^3$, it would be $3.650.00, and at $10^4$, we would be making $36,500.00 a year. Of all of the preceding figures, the one that most closely matches the estimated $24,498 USD per capita income for England for the year 2000, is the latest.

This means today's $10^4$ Britons—as referred to a prehistoric population of 5000 hunter-gatherers—enjoy a standard of living that is also $10^4$ times the same reference. Now, $10^4$ multiplied by $10^4$, equals to $10^8$ (one hundred million). So, that is how much the territory of England would have been made to overproduce above the chosen prehistoric level.

We will now use the previous reasoning to fix our only mathematical expression for good, eliminating the nonsense of assuming human populations as remaining constant within any territory, or the entire world.

The natural resources within the English territory, multiplied by the technology currently in use by its population, translate into a number of goods and services, the sum of which is reducible to monetary units, expressing in fact, their GNP. The English GNP, when divided among its population, results in their average per capita income, which in turn, is the monetary expression of their standard of living. We would state this by writing:

$$\frac{NrT}{P} = SL$$

This is a crude (and yet valid) law, which shows the standard of living, represented by $SL$, as a function of the variables on the left side of the expression. Increasing the natural resources, the power of the technology in use, or both, will result in a bigger output pulling up the figure of the standard of living. Conversely, increasing the population will have the opposite effect, diminishing the figure for the standard of living. (The most observing reader will notice that in this last expression, the positions between the dividend and the divisor have switched places. This was necessary in order to express the per capita income in the usual way, that is, as the quotient of a given output divided by a certain number of population, and not vice versa.)

Now, is there any use we can find for this crude law? I will show so, for it holds much more than meets the eye. For instance, on past lines we characterized the process of developing technology as being a so simple one, that it almost seemed inevitable for all human groups to have produced technology in fairly the same degrees, at fairly the same times. But we know different. No matter what time frame the select, we will notice that there have always been more advanced groups coexisting with others much less-developed. Why?

# PART TWO

# THE HISTORY OF THE PAST

# 4
# AN HYPOTETICAL PREHISTORIC SCENARIO

## Random Differentiation

Once I knew there was no way for any human group to escape the fixed relationship between the variables I had identified, I tried to imagine how was that they could undergo any changes on their own. Being all the variables inextricably related, all I needed to do to see the others affected was to induce a change in just one of them. Thus, this is what I devised, though at a time I was not familiar with the fact that hunter-gatherer populations tend to remain stable.

I supposed some prehistoric group "A," living near the mouth of a quiet river. This group would make its living out of the vegetable food in the their territory, as well as on small volatile, terrestrial and aquatic preys. I then supposed nature in this area being extraordinarily generous through the course of several generations, so that the population of the group would have been inadvertently growing, until it doubled.

With the return of the natural conditions to its average level, only half the population could be sustained, meaning all of the group's population would suffer. Under such circumstances, frictions would arise.

Two fractions would be created by this "political" turmoil. One leader would urge the group to move up to some nearby hills, where according to legend, bigger prey abounds. A second leader would be of the opinion to ask the gods for mercy, and wait. After some incident, the group would split. While group "AA" stays, group "AB" starts its journey up the hills.

Given these circumstances, group "AB" would probably perish. For the sake of this example, we will suppose that while only 1 in 10,000 groups in the position of the "AB" would escape extinction, this occasion was precisely one of the rare fortunate ones.

So, group "AB" experiences the first deaths within days of having started their adventure up the hills. Bigger prey, like the predicted, is seen, but the group lacks the knowledge and tools to hunt them. Gathering activities performed by the women (which normally provide most of the food) yield poor results, since the new territory's plants are unknown to them. All the male hunters can do is to catch small animals once in a while. Famished, the group keeps following the bigger prey until they find a quiet lake resembling their original settlement. There are lots of fish, as well as small terrestrial and volatile preys.

Unexpectedly, the group is saved by this fortunate finding. Later on, however, they insist on hunting the bigger animals, until they succeed. They now have plenty of meat food, and they have identified too the edible plants in their new lands. Group "AB" recovers from the expedition's casualties, regaining its original size, and then doubles in numbers, living nevertheless, under much better conditions than they originally did. Because any of the groups "AA" and "AB" could be in the position of the other, we can say that differentiation among them took place randomly.

I will now analyze other important implications of this imaginary exercise.

## Arising of New Ways of Life

Firstly, we should notice that the rule valid for all natural species concerning the balance between their populations and the resources available in nature, was preserved. All excess food was translated straightforwardly into population, being that way how the parent group "A" doubled its size, without developing a new standard of living.

With the return of the average conditions, the excess population cannot be sustained unless new territories are invaded, technology is developed, or both. As supposed, new territories were occupied, but had not the group "AB" developed technology, it would have remained as a mere duplicate of the original group "A," or the one that took its place, the "AA." Since we supposed that group "AB" developed technology, a further increase in population was made possible. Finally, only because of the creation of technology, group "AB" was able to raise its living standards.

The former means that only the groups that develop (or assimilate) technology, can opt for new ways of life characterized not only by a greater abundance of previously known goods, but especially, by the appearance of new ones.

At this point, however, we must notice that the natural rule no longer applies. In order for any living standards to be raised, it is necessary to suppose that part of the productive possibilities of any groups are devoted to that end, for further increases of population would effectively prevent this effect from happening.

This opens the disconcerting question of how a group "knows" when to stop growing in numbers. Because the answer of this question is neither obvious nor immediate, we shall leave it for later chapters. For now, in order to exemplify the possible different equilibriums between population and standard of living, we can think of three different behaviors. The least "progressive" group would continue growing in numbers within its new productive possibilities, keeping roughly the same standard of living it had before. A medium "progressive" group would devote part of its enhanced capabilities to sustain more population, and part to let all the population enjoy a higher standard of life. Finally, the most "progressive" group imaginable, would apply the entirety of its new productive capabilities exclusively to live better, remaining stable in numbers. (As we shall see, there is a fourth possibility, as some contemporary developed nations show a steady improvement of their living standards, while shrinking in population numbers.)

## Extinction of the Original Ways of Life

Aside from the previous, we should note that just one of the two groups experienced all the changes. After group "AA" lost its excess population, all pressure upon it vanished, thus it remained unchanged. On the other hand, all of the four indicators of group "AB" experienced a positive increase in value. Because of its adventure, group "AB" uses new and more effective technology, holds more population, lives better, and occupies a greater extension of land. (In many cases throughout these lines, the natural resources under the control of a group will be identified with the territory held by it.)

Therefore, as stated, we now have two different groups evolved from a common ancestor, showing nevertheless, a different degree of development. Being the group "AB" more populous and extended, should we repeat for both groups "AA" and "AB," the same events supposed for the original group "A," the greatest probability of producing more groups descended from their common branch, would be on the side of group "AB." Thus, we could imagine a series of groups "$AB_1...AB_n$" all descended from the "AB" group. Of these new groups, a majority would perish, a smaller proportion would survive as replicas of group "AB," and just a few, or only one, would reproduce its successful feat.

By adding more, and more advanced groups, the possibility of extinction (or assimilation) would be more likely on the side of the lesser advanced groups, with isolation being the only factor acting in favor of their preservation. On the long run, however, isolation would be less and less a possibility, thus resulting in the extinction of the less-developed, or more ancient ways of life. Similarly, representing with circumferences the areas occupied by the different groups (related or not), any overlapping of the perimeters would result in disputed territories, increasing the chance of clashes.

## Technological Transference

Abrupt differences in development would be, however, no guarantee for the continuity of the most advanced groups. While the more advanced groups could succeed a great number of times in destroying, decimating, subduing or assimilating lesser developed rivals, some of these less-developed groups could be restoring its population while learning from the strengths of the more advanced society. This implies technology being easily transferable. The mere contact between two groups of different degree of development enables the least developed one to copy or assimilate the more advanced means of the neighbor (as a strange example, some prehistoric stone tools are known to be replicas of the same bronze instruments).

This transferal mechanism will prove useful in explaining the fall and displacement of great powers by the action of groups of humbler origins, regardless the first being a loathed rival or the parental society itself. The success of a previously less-developed group in subduing a more advanced one, equally implies the extinction of the most ancient or less-advanced ways of life, for the previously less-developed group could not remain unchanged precisely in those characteristics marking it as less-developed.

Other consequences implied in this exercise are as follows.

We assumed population could increase under natural periods of unusual abundance, this is, without developing technology. Yet, for this increase to become a permanent addition, it was necessary to suppose new lands were invaded, technology was developed, or both. But, if in the long run, we think of territories remaining constant (as in the case of England), it will be only by developing technology that any permanent population additions will be made possible.

## Demographic-Technologic Cycles

Now, if we consider the resulting groups being bigger (and not just more), such groups would be exposed to greater or new necessities, which, in turn, could be solved only by developing more technology. What we have here is a demographic-technologic cycle, with either factor pulling the other. For instance, a group possessing a small and stable population would seldom experience greater or new necessities, thus a concept such as "aqueduct" would not have any meaning. On the other hand, any groups succeeding in developing a technology such as agriculture, for example, would hold greater populations. These particular groups, because of their success, would eventually face the exhaustion of some of their basic resources such as the water easily available. Under those circumstances, an inexistent structure, an aqueduct, would be required.

Again, the success in the construction of a small aqueduct would solve the problem, thus letting the population keep its upward tendency. As a result, through the course of the generations we should be able to observe successive groups, besides developing larger and more sophisticated aqueduct systems, experiencing other new problems as well, such as say, that of sewage, all of this implying the development of gradually more complex and specialized structures.

# 5

# TOYNBEE'S MODEL OF HISTORY

## Toynbee's Twenty-One Civilizations

As mentioned at the beginning of these lines, between 1934 and 1961, the English professor Arnold Joseph Toynbee wrote a monumental work of 10 volumes, under the title of *"A Study of History."* Before Toynbee's effort was finished, a colleague and friend of him, D.C. Somervell, started to write an abridgement that reduced the first six volumes from over 3000 to 565 pages. But Somervell had the vision to produce an abridgement of the abridgement, thus compressing the first six volumes to only 25 pages. Toynbee had a powerful reason to write to such an extent.

While examining the whole of the human history, the historian stumbled with the fact that there were a number of different historical societies, the majority of which were already "dead." Toynbee identified 21 different historical civilizations: 1) the Western, 2) the Orthodox-

Byzantine, 3) the Orthodox-Russian, 4) the Iranic, 5) the Arabic, 6) the Hindu, 7) the Chinese, 8) the Korean-Japanese, 9) the Hellenic, 10) the Syriac, 11) the Indic, 12) the Sinic, 13) the Minoan, 14) the Sumeric, 15) the Hittite, 16) the Babylonic, 17) the Egyptiac, 18) the Andean, 19) the Mexic, 20) the Yucatec, 21) and the Mayan.

Of those civilizations still "alive," Toynbee considered all of them, except for his own, the Western civilization, as showing evident symptoms of decay, identifying such symptoms with their "breakdown." Determined to complete a picture that not only included the breakdown and disintegration of the civilizations, he embarked on the complementary study of their genesis and growth.

The similarities between some names of Toynbee's 21 civilizations are due to filiation-relationships. The Hindu civilization is descended from the Indic, in the same way the Western is the offspring of the Hellenic. Should one ask where the Roman Empire fits, the answer is that it belongs to the Hellenic civilization or "Greco-Roman," as Toynbee also calls it.

It is here where we find the first weakness of the Toynbeean method. While naming his 21 civilizations, Toynbee mentions another one, the Islamic, noting that the Iranic and the Arabic societies are now united into this one. What does this mean? Should we reduce the figure of 21 civilizations down to twenty because of the fusion of these two? Or, should we better rename the two societies as the "Iranic-Islamic" and the "Arabic-Islamic" (as Toynbee also refers to them), in order to keep the number of 21 societies a fixed one?

Evidently, a definitive partition of the humanity into any number of distinct and well-differentiated historical societies, is an impossible task. One should better pay attention to what Darwin and Wallace had to say about the same problem. When faced with the monumental task of classifying natural life, both biologists came to the conclusion that all divisions were arbitrary. The following lines belong to Darwin's *"Origin"*:

"The forms which possess in some considerable degree the character of species, but which are so closely similar to other forms...are in several respects the most important for us...Mr. H.C. Watson... has marked for me 182 British plants, which are generally considered as varieties, but which have all been ranked by botanists as species... Under genera, including the most polymorphic forms, Mr. Babington gives 251 species, whereas Mr. Bentham gives only 112—a difference of 139 doubtful forms!... Mr. Wallace, in several valuable papers on the various animals, especially on the Lepidoptera, inhabiting the islands of the great Malayan Archipelago, shows that they may be classed under four heads...but as they do not differ from each other by strongly marked and important characters, "there is no possible test but individual opinion to determine which of them shall be considered as species and which as varieties."... I look at the term species as one arbitrarily given, for the sake of convenience, to a set of individuals closely resembling each other, and that it does not essentially differ from the term variety, which is given to less distinct and more fluctuating forms. The term variety, again, in comparison with mere individual differences, is also applied arbitrarily, for convenience' sake."[11]

Oddly enough, Toynbee makes use of the terms "species" and "genus" in reference to his partitions of the human kind, this time, to differentiate between the societies he ranks as civilized, and the primitive ones. The following lines belong to his "*Study*":

"Societies which are 'intelligible fields of study' are a genus within which our twenty-one representatives constitute one particular species. Societies of this species are commonly called civilizations, to distinguish them from primitive societies which are also 'intelligible fields of study' and which form another, in fact *the* other, species within this genus"[12]

In regard to "the other species," the primitive societies, Toynbee mentions that in 1915 three Western anthropologists were able to identify over 650, most of them alive at that time. Toynbee also acknowledges that, although there is no way to estimate the number of primitive societies that came into and passed out of existence since man first became human, they overwhelmingly outnumber his 21 civilized societies. In spite of this, he discards primitive societies from the scope of his study. He reasons that primitive societies do not weigh in terms of population, for any of his true civilized ones has embraced more human beings than all of the primitive societies together since the appearance of the human race.

Within the civilized status, Toynbee also contemplates other possibilities, such as those of the "aborted" and the "arrested" civilizations. The degree of civilization is too an issue. Toynbee recognizes other societies coexisting with his true civilized ones, which are barbaric, causing a recurring "Völkerwanderung" (migration of peoples), their historic role being to sting the spirit of his civilized societies, challenging them.

## Toynbee's Four Phases

The former classification difficulties are but trifle objections when compared to the main inconsistency of the Toynbeean method. Toynbee resorts to different mechanisms while trying to explain the four phases his civilizations go through.

The genesis of a civilization is the product of the successful response to a challenge posed by nature. The growth is also due to a successful response to a series of successive challenges, and this time the challenges coming within the society itself. The breakdown happens by the failure of the creative power of the creative minorities, leading to the loss of unity of the civilized group. Following this loss of unity, disintegration, the schism of the social body, happens, meaning the society splits into three fractions, a dominant minority, an internal proletariat and an external proletariat (an alternative to disintegration is the "petrifaction" of the society).

Thus, while his first two phases respond to his principle of "challenge-and-response," the last two have more to do with an obscure process of internal decay. While the Toynbeean method is unacceptable, his work renders two valuable findings. The cycle Toynbee conceived is what I call a historic regularity, a phenomenon that reappears regardless of historical eras and geographies, though I would rather try to describe it in much simpler terms such as the rise, growth, decline, and disappearance of historical societies. A second finding, which I regard as useful, is Toynbee's "challenge-and-response" principle. We will now try to adapt these two Toynbeean elements (the four-phase cycle, and his "challenge-and-response" principle) to our own views.

## Challenge-and-Response Principle

The genesis of a civilization, by means of successfully reacting to a challenge posed by nature, resembles quite closely the hardships we supposed group "AB" had to endure. So we can regard Toynbee's principle of "challenge-and-response" (or its absence) as important in explaining the condition of different groups (for example, group "AB" having varied, versus group "AA" having remained the same), except that Toynbee's conception of this principle has a peculiarity.

According to the historian, within the phase of the geneses of civilizations, challenges must assume a "golden mean" between an excess of rigor and a lack of it, for an insufficient challenge can fail in stimulating the challenged part, while an excessive one might break its spirit. In our case, we will not need a "golden mean." Our genesis mechanism is a technologic-demographic cycle that works under a probabilistic scheme. For instance, for the only time group "AB" succeeded, we considered other 9,999 just like it perished. Thus, for our mechanism to produce the rise of a civilization (or generate gradually more advanced societies) we only have to suppose the same events repeating enough times during the course of many generations.

Should someone argue that the Toynbeean "golden mean" is just another way to depict this probabilistic scheme (with the excessive challenge being the cause of the extinction of our 9,999 supposed groups, the insufficient challenge being the cause of the stagnation of groups like the "AA," and the "golden mean" being the reason behind the success of group "AB"), we would then accept the two views as being formally the same. If, however, Toynbee's "golden mean" remains characterized in such a peculiar way that cannot be reconciled with our probabilistic approach, we would then be favoring our own views.

In regards to the growths of civilizations, Toynbee considers them not as being the result of the success of the civilized group over external factors, such as their mastering of the environment (by technological means), their geographic expansion, or their control over other peoples (by military means). Instead, Toynbee views the growths of civilizations as the consequence of the "self-determination" of the civilized groups, which are guided to this end by the action of creative individuals or creative minorities.

These peculiar concepts stand in the way of our much simpler model. For any group to grow, all we will be invoking is again, the action of our demographic-technologic cycle. As stated before, the development or assimilation of technology, because of enabling population growth, eventually leads to the appearance of new needs that in turn, can be solved only by further technological developments.

Under this conception, any particular society's growth process can be too influenced by chance. For instance, of two warring groups, one could be the first to develop the most effective means of transportation, weaponry, strategy, etc., but be defeated by the other because of say, an epidemic. On the long run, however, this process is not governed by chance at all. Continuing with the same example, if the warring group initially favored by a blow of luck does not do anything to enhance its capabilities, nothing will prevent the one previously defeated rising again and using its superior means to reverse the original outcome, eventually toppling the backwards group for good.

Now, what can lead a successful group, one that has effectively coped with challenge after challenge, to its breakdown and disintegration (or decline and disappearance)? Before addressing these questions, we will first review some more of Toynbee's peculiar conceptions of the growth, breakdown and disintegration processes.

According to Toynbee, the growth of a civilization is accomplished by the action of creative individuals or small minorities that succeed first, in achieving their own inspiration or discoveries, and later, in making the rest of the society following them in a collective act of "mimesis" (imitation). But mimesis, according to the historian, has its dangers. The leaders can become infected by its mechanical nature, thus losing their creative power (and end imitating their imitators), or they can impatiently exchange persuasion by the whip of compulsion. The creative minorities are thus turned into mere dominant minorities, with the former disciples becoming an alienated proletariat. Such are the internal changes Toynbee identifies as the breakdown, with the disintegration seeming to be a more severe stage of the breakdown, characterized by the schism of the social body, meaning its internal splitting, and not the actual "death" or extinction of the civilization.

For our purposes, we shall replace the breakdown with the stabilization of the society. In fact, in a note of his own at the end of the Chapter XV of the *"Study,"* D.C. Somervell equates the breakdown of a civilization to the termination of its period of growth. In very much the same way, the cases of disappearance or extinction of historical societies are better understood in terms of the population of any societies being subdued and eventually assimilated by other groups.

So, our most immediate question, is that of how a society or civilization stops growing and stabilizes, as they never thrive indefinitely in population numbers and technological means. In order to start us in this analysis, we will borrow from Malthus.

We can infer after Malthus that the productive possibilities of any country are limited, the nature of the limiting factors being represented by the finite product of the multiplication of its resources by its technology. (Even if technology in the long run enables such amazing yields as $10^8$, the period associated to this figure is about 10,000 years long, with the better part of the amazing increases in productivity having appeared in just the last couple of centuries. Besides, technological limitations are always present, otherwise, today cancer would not kill us, and traffic jams would not annoy us.)

Further, if the productive possibilities of any economic systems are limited, then it follows that every historical society—having exploited its lands and resources to a maximum—had to stop growing in population unless it accepted to survive under increasingly lowered standards. Theoretically, this situation chances the possibility of eventually reaching the minimum caloric consumption needed to sustain a human organism alive. What we have got us here is an absolute limit, one that cannot be broken no matter how hard we try.

## Opposed Demographical Behaviors

The observation of some contemporary societies, however, will not let us affirm the applicability of such an absolute limit. Some of the most advanced societies of our time, belonging to the European Union, have formidable productive apparatuses, while showing a steady decrease in their populations. In fact, their problem is not scarcity, but the exact opposite, overproduction. Dumping practices (selling produce under its market value or even its production costs) is expressly forbidden within the enlarged borders of the Union. The overproduction problem is so acute, however, that farmers still block roads at the national borders to protest or impede the entry of produce that according to their perception or knowledge, has been unfairly subsidized by the country of origin.

In the industrial sector, in order not to shutdown automobile plants, thus dismissing thousands of workers, some European automakers are proposing their unions the reduction of the working shifts. The proposal has, in turn, provoked an irate reaction as all of the workers will see their wages proportionally diminished. In other cases, permanent closures are inevitable, so that angry demonstrations of the dismissed workers in one union country take place in front of the embassy of the investor country, also a member of the Union.

At the same time, many underdeveloped countries with insufficient productive systems are, in spite of their condition, showing a steady increase in their population. This state of things seems to be contradictory. The countries in the best position to accommodate greater population numbers (with their economies, so to speak, begging for a stronger demand), show stationary or decreasing populations, while the countries that should be keeping under a strict leash their demographic growth, seem to be flirting with disaster.

But then, if productive limitations are apparently not the factor containing demographic expansion, we will have to further look for an alternative explanation.

# 6
# WAR

## Early Stabilization

In Walt Disney's 1963 movie *"The Sword on the Stone,"* Wart, future king of England, holds a conversation with magician Merlin and his owl Archimedes, in regards to Merlin's abilities to foresee the future. From a dusty corner of his dwelling, Merlin brings a scale model of a locomotive, causing it to propel itself with a bit of hot tea poured in its interior. As Wart, marveled, acknowledges Merlin's wisdom, the magician replies with the observation that the machine will not be invented in centuries.

With the same kind of amazement as Wart's, one could ask oneself what inventions correspond to what ages, and why. A noted French researcher[13] dealing with the subject of the evolution of technology, has pointed out that the ancient Greeks had neither the means nor the necessity for developing properly working steam engines. (The first ancestor of these devices was the aeolipile, a metal sphere that revolved on its axis due to the steam exhausted through two small opposite curved tubes attached to it, thought to be invented by the

Greek mathematician Heron of Alexandria, approximately between the years 20 and 62 A.D.)

The same reasons—lack of both means and necessity—would explain why the Greco-Roman world did not develop a mechanized industrialism. But this explanation looks only half true. Lacking the technological means for building a locomotive is certainly a good reason to prevent its development, but on the other hand, even if the technology is available, the locomotive is still not produced unless necessity prevails.

In the Greco-Roman world, when machines were needed for the purpose of war, they were rapidly developed. Clever, complex and powerful devices such as dented wheels, catapults, crossbows, battering rams and moving towers, were as diligently put to work during wartimes, as they were ignored later for all civilian purposes. Therefore, while the Greco-Roman world had indeed some technological means to start a crude form of mechanical industrialism, what it lacked completely, was the necessity to develop it. Thus, technological advancement is in many cases, better understood in terms of existing needs, rather than in terms of existing means.

As we now see, the demographic growth of ancient societies such as the Greek and the Roman, seems to have stopped long before exhausting both their resources and technological possibilities, a fact that renders or Malthusian "absolute limit" inapplicable even for remote eras.

In recent times, too, any device or technique that does not find a use remains (as Heron's aeolipile), as a mere curiosity belonging in a scientist's laboratory or a museum. Conversely, when an even imperfect technique shows immediate possibilities for practical use, it is quickly developed. In 1895, the German scientist Wilhelm Conrad Röentgen discovered by accident the X-rays, the first radiographs being accidentally produced by the same scientist, since X-ray capabilities for exposing photographic plates were unknown even for him.

As soon as 1913 (18 years later), the American physicist William D. Coolidge was able to perfect an emitting device. On the other hand, the photoelectric effect, known at least since 1883 (12 years before the X-rays) when the first photovoltaic cell was invented, was a worthless energy source until the need to produce electricity in such remote places as the outer space, where artificial satellites now abound, was experienced.

## The Effects of War Pressures on Technological Development

Since war pressures are always more severe than civilian ones, it is fair so say that the technologic potential of any society at any time, is best revealed at wartimes. War (hot or cold) is also an excellent example of how easily technology is permeated between different human groups.

In peacetimes, technology is assimilated or reproduced by the mere contact or closeness between groups. But in wartimes, even the highest degree of secrecy cannot impede technology replication. The detonation of two atomic bombs over Japan in 1945 by the United States, "informed" the Russians on the exact degree of the Americans' advancement, ultimately, confirming the feasibility of the development of such a weapon, and revealing such data as the size of its destructive capabilities. This "caused" as soon as 1949—4 years later—the first successful replication of an atomic bomb on the side of the Soviets. (According to most of their scientists' guesses and intelligence sources, the United States did not expect the Soviet Union to become a nuclear power for decades after their first public demonstration of 1945, thus, forecasts estimating the Soviets as having the bomb by the mid-1960s, were regarded as exaggerated.)

Russia, a much less-advanced country, would eventually surpass briefly the United States' nuclear capability by developing the first portable hydrogen bomb. This much more powerful fusion bomb requires the detonation of a fission (uranium) bomb, in order to reach the temperatures and pressures necessary to start a fusion reaction (of hydrogen), thus consisting of two bombs in one. Shortly after, the United States, on November 1, 1952, detonated an H-bomb contained in a massive building. The explosion annihilated not only the building itself but also an entire isle on the Enewetak Atoll in the Pacific Ocean. In less than a year on August 12, 1953, the Russians were able to explode the same weapon in mid-air.

The previous shows us that any society that can be characterized as advanced or developed, has a wealth of both resources and technology that remain largely unused, a fact that can be seen under the form of economies that are able (or cannot avoid) to overproduce.

These unused capabilities become evident under circumstances of extreme pressure, such as war, when they find an immediate use. But extreme pressure not only reveals the size of the existing unused capabilities as they are put to work. Extreme and prolonged pressure also unleashes the unknown, far-reaching portion of these capabilities, with big differences in development not being a definitive indicator of what a country or society can do.

Another good example for this, is the space exploration race. The Soviets, with a lot less resources than the United States, were able to put the first artificial satellite in orbit. This came as a shock, for the United States was the first in publicly announcing on July 29, 1955, its own Vanguard satellite program. After two years of an intense campaign of information on behalf of the United States' program, the Russians suddenly informed the successful launching of the first Sputnik, on October 4, 1957.

The United States, who had the help of German physicist Wernher Von Braun, head of team that developed the liquid-fuel supersonic V-2 rocket used for bombarding England in the late Second World War, was stunned to learn Sputnik 1 weighed 84 kg. (As the last stage of the propelling rocket was put in orbit too, total orbiting mass was 4000 kg.) Meanwhile the Vanguard weight was only of 1.48 kg.

Before the United States could react, a Sputnik 2 was launched one month later on November 3, 1957. This time the satellite's weight alone was over 500 kg., carrying a living animal, a female dog named Laika. After an unsuccessful attempt carried out by the Vanguard team on December 6, 1957, a different team from the United States was able to launch the Explorer 1 on January 31, 1958, the satellite mass being 8.5 kg, or 14 kg, if including the weight of the engine.

Thus, as stated, technological breakthroughs are more likely to be produced under severe need, and, as the examples of the United States versus the Soviet Union competition shows, there is no way to tell for sure what country will be the first to develop any given technology. (The space race contest was never a peaceful or scientific one, as we are commonly led to believe. In fact, the military balance between the United States and the Soviets was at stake.)

How should we characterize war then, as a collateral and undesirable effect of progress? As a flaw in human nature, as a historical "perversion" as Toynbee saw it? Or is war not only unavoidable but necessary under our particular kind of evolution?

## The Nature of War

Not mattering how we choose to depict the concept, war, which was already implied in our demographic-technologic expansive model, has been a constant phenomena throughout our recorded history, and in many cases, the direct cause of the "death" of many societies. So, we need to clearly identify what are the factors that successively render the phenomenon possible, later make it more probable, and finally gives it its recurrent nature.

In order to start our analysis, we shall not begin with our species (the only one where the phenomenon is known to occur), but we will rather focus on nature. Thanks chiefly to the work of ethologists, scientists specializing in animal behavior, we know that there are two main forms of aggression. The interespecific aggression is the one occurring between different species, and encompasses predation, defense, and that directed against competitors of scarce resources such as food or water. The intraspecific aggression is the one that happens among the individuals of the same species. It is observed in all vertebrates, and it is due to the fact that individuals of the same species have to compete for the same kind of resources such as food, mate and dwelling.

For our purposes, this second variant of aggression is the more important. Because combat between two individuals of the same species is dangerous, there are natural mechanisms that limit the extent of the aggression. Establishing well-defined territories reduces the frequency of combats to border disputes. Ritualization of combat also operates. Under such form of aggression both the challenging and the challenged individuals engage in fights without harming each other seriously. This produces a winner and loser and avoids injuries that could predispose them to predation by members of other species. In addition to these limiting mechanisms, there are others that end aggression. The individual that gives up produces a clear signal indicating its defeat, such as exposing a vulnerable part to the opponent.

All of the former tells us aggression is either necessary to survive in a highly competed environment, or its unavoidable consequence. Should an individual lose completely its capabilities to show an aggressive behavior, it would surely famish, find no dwelling place, remain without a mate, or be incapable of defending its offspring or group.

We will now observe man, though not in civilized societies.

As it is easy to confirm, aggression in contemporary hunter-gatherer societies is a rare phenomenon. Forms or ritualized combat among humans have also been observed. In the 19th century, between African tribes, rival parties would meet at the common border, facing each other, producing yells, insults, and threatening gestures such as the raising and waving of their weapons in defiance. Missiles such as stones, sticks, arrows or spears were thrown, though most landing in the area between the two fronts, thus, rarely injuring anyone.

After sufficiently prolonging these kind of behavior, the group most impressed by the number or force of the opponent would retire from the "battle" ground, thus accepting the reduction of their territory to the "enemy." Between contemporary nomads, the best tactic is still to flee away from any threats. In regards to individual disputes, aggression and its consequences are limited in a number of ways, as observed by anthropologists:

> "Man A threw a boomerang with just the right speed so that man B (who had stolen A's wife) could dodge my moving fast. Then they ran at one another, knives in hand, dropped to their knees, and man A proceeded to make a short slash across man B's chest, just deep enough to draw blood and exact blood vengeance. That was the end of the feud."[14]

All of the previous tells us, however, that competence and aggression between individuals and groups still take place among the least populated and less technologically advanced societies of our age. The only aspect that varies significantly within civilized societies is scale. Indicators such as the number of casualties, the frequency and duration of the confrontations, and the resources devoted to them, support this affirmation.

Starting with the demographic aspect, it is population growth that makes contact between two different groups possible. Closer and more frequent contacts render borders first necessary, and later useless. Similarly, small clashes evolve into larger and more violent confrontations where the loss of life is inevitable. Only the ever-growing size of populations produces the kind of pressure that makes these fights possible. No group would take seriously the "threat" of a weak and small neighbor.

Technology, independently from its major contribution, which is to enable population growth, also plays an important factor. No war can be waged without weapons, devices specifically designed to kill—and not only to "neutralize" as it is sometimes euphemistically said—the enemy. As one military (I believe American) once stated, no soldier will be rendering its country a great service by dying for it, but rather, by causing enemy soldiers to die for theirs'. It is technology then, what enables massive destruction, for without it wars would be reduced to stone fights, or man-to-man combats with objects such as sticks taking the place of the weapons that typify war. Surely, man-to-man fights can end in death, but body counts on the scale of thousands or even hundreds, are hard to imagine this way.

When considering the role of the standard of living, the most improbable feature promoting war makes its appearance. Every war is a contest, and behind any contest there is a prize. It is only by comparison, that two groups can view themselves as rich or poor, and it is only by this relative condition of richness or poorness, that the idea of conquest can have a meaning.

The utility of conquest is obvious. The fastest way to improve the living standard of a population is by means of the appropriation or control of the neighbor's resources or liberties. Differences in the technological level are no obstacle for the phenomenon to occur in any direction. To subdue a neighbor with a comparable degree of development implies the benefit of the winner, with the same effect being produced by one group's appropriating of the lands or resources of a lesser developed rival or neighbor. Again, taking over a more advanced group renders the same outcome. The most illustrative examples about the barbarian's push against Europe coming from Malthus denote much more greed and glory seeking than hunger. The following lines belong to his "Essay":

"Want was the goad that drove the Scythian shepherds from their native haunts, like so many famished wolves in search of prey. Set in motion by this all-powerful cause, clouds of Barbarians seemed to collect from all points of the Northern Hemisphere. Gathering fresh darkness and terror as they rolled on, the congregated bodies at length obscured the sun of Italy and sunk the whole world in universal night."

"Young scions were then pushed out from the parent-stock and instructed to explore fresh regions and to gain happier seats for themselves by their swords. 'The world was all before them where to choose.' Restless from present distress, flushed with the hope of fairer prospects, and animated with the spirit of hardy enterprise, these daring adventurers were likely to become formidable adversaries to all who opposed them. The peaceful inhabitants of the countries on which they rushed could not long withstand the energy of men acting under such powerful motives of exertion."[15]

Any wars that are not definable as conquer-oriented, as those prompted by nationalist, independent, libertarian or religious feelings, seek the same effects by means of the suppression of any burdens, threats, tributes, taxation, or impositions. In short, all wars seek the improvement of the condition of a group.

So it happens in the cases of internal fracture, when two groups within a same nation or society struggle against each other, for the defeat of one will imply the benefit of the winner.

The role of "psychological" needs such as "liberty" deserve a special consideration. To fulfill his mission as the leash against the enemy, freedom fighters and/or religious, political, or ethnic warriors suffer deprivations of pay, housing, medical and social security, etc. They put their liberty and lives at stake, and even sacrifice themselves in suicidal attacks.

Thus, the psychological component of many of our needs is more important than it may seem at first sight. For example, how much money is donated throughout the world to religious organizations? What is the utility or function of such organizations? What product or service do they provide in exchange for the public's generous contributions? If we discard the improvement of the individual's condition after passing away as the main goal behind his or her donations, we are left but with a few answers.

Having noted this, for our purposes, trying to distinguish between "real" and merely "psychological" needs is fruitless, because the same effects will be produced. Or, in other words, the mere perception, by an individual or a group of a necessity, will turn such need it into a real one.

Synthesizing, war is only the most visible and extreme form of competition pervading all levels of animal life, including humans. War does not happen at all in nature, or it is rare among the least developed or more primitive human societies, because populations do not thrive, technological means are nonexistent or low, and there are no distinct benefits that can be obtained by means of a violent and unrestricted confrontation.

# 7
# THE ANCIENT EGYPT, AN EXTINCT SOCIETY

## The Added Effects of Competition

Few facts impressed me as a schoolboy as much as the disappearance of the ancient Egyptians. My first General History book devoted one of its first chapters to them, the reproduced images of their monumental structures and rich art, being the cause of my amazement. I was very disappointed later by the fact that besides that only chapter devoted to describe their feats, no further mention of them was made.

Where had they gone?

Our very simple model of history—one that explains the emergence of ever more advanced societies in terms of an expansive demographic-technologic cycle that implies war, though still lacking a stabilizing mechanism—can make plain the downfall of advanced civilizations.

Now that we have characterized war as the most extreme form of competition between different human societies, one can see how the expansive quality of an expansive-only model produces the competitive pressure that extinguishes, tears down, or disintegrates civilizations.

Under isolation, no extinction or discontinuity of a prosperous, well-established society can be explained, and the few remaining hunter-gatherer societies preserved until present times, sustains this affirmation. Similarly, the ancient Egypt was not only self-sufficient, but had the typical surplus economy we see today in advanced nations.

So, if by the time the ancient Egypt thrived, other societies had remained stationary, the land of the Pharaohs would still exist today, unchanged. A brief "biography" of the ancient Egypt shows the "cause of death" being indisputably the action of other groups. Let us take a look to the following summary.

Old Kingdom (2755-2181 B.C.) 3rd to 6th Dynasties show five centuries of uninterrupted progress and splendor, capitol city is in Memphis; Giza pyramids are constructed, military incursions in Asia take place.

First intermediate period: internal struggle, the 7th and 8th Dynasties reign only for 25 years; under the 9th and 10th dynasties, political power is exerted by the nomarchs (district governors); rival nomarchs from the south establish the 11th Dynasty with capitol city in Thebes (in the south).

Middle Kingdom (2134-1784 B.C.) the 11th and 12th Dynasties regain power and place their capitol city mainly in Thebes, fortresses in Nubia are erected, governors to Palestine and Syria are sent, campaigns against Libya are waged.

Second intermediate period: the 13th dynasty loses control over the Delta, where a 14th independent dynasty is established; the Hyksos—Semitic peoples that introduced the horse to Egypt—invade and establish the 15th dynasty with capitol city in Avaris; a 16th Dynasty coexists in the del Delta and the Middle Egypt as subsidiaries of the Hyksos; the 17th Dynasty, Theban, subdues the Hyksos reuniting Egypt.

New Kingdom (1570-1070 B.C.) the 18th through 20th Dynasties expand over Nubia and Palestine, construct on Karnack and wage new campaigns against the Hittites, Syrian, Palestine, and Libyan; Abu Simbel is built.

Third intermediate period: 21st to 24th Dynasties reign; the 21st is Libyan; the 23rd and 24th are contemporary to the 22nd; the 25th Dynasty which is Kushite, is too contemporary with Dynasties 22nd to 24th.

Late period: the 25th Dynasty is dethroned by the Assyrians, the 26th recovers the country briefly but the Persians invade and establish the 27th dynasty; Dynasties 28th to 30th are again Egyptian, but the 30th the last of native origin, as the Persians invade and establish the 31st Dynasty.

Hellenistic and Roman Period: in 332 B.C., Alexander the Great ends Persian domination, starting the Ptolemaic (Greek) Dynasties that Hellenize Egypt; last Ptolemaic ruler is Cleopatra, who dies in 30 B.C.

Roman-Byzantine period: seven centuries of domination Christianize Egypt; there is a Persian invasion on 616. The Arab invasion of 642 opens the Caliphates period and within two centuries, by the time of the Abbasids (750-868), the population speaks Arab and their religion becomes Islamic. The Copt, a language derived from the ancient Egyptian, is preserved only for Christian liturgics.

And, from then on, Egypt develops into the modern Arab nation we all know.

As we can clearly see in the previous summary, the disintegration, disappearance or extinction of historical societies is caused by the competitive action of other groups. As stated, what Toynbee conceived as his "disintegration" stage is merely a chaotic state of affairs within a split society that, nevertheless, does not deprive it of the characteristic features identifying the society as one different to any other.

However, when any society is gradually stripped of its language, customs, religion and social organization, it becomes harder to acknowledge it as a unit differing to that of the society or societies that have subdued it or assimilated it.

The first stages of the Egyptian "life," reveal a steady growth and expansion over its neighbors, a phase which can be surely correlated with a strong Egyptian demographic growth. Later on, we see the action of some of these neighbors or even newcomers, pushing against Egyptian sovereignty, a fact that indicates us both the Egyptian population having stabilized, and that of their competitors having augmented.

In further stages, the local rulers are less and less in control, having to share their own territories with intruders. Finally, the main struggling parties within Egypt are not Egyptian, but the different peoples trying to hold their grip on the Egyptian people and lands. The last invader just finishes the process, kicking out all of the other intruders, keeping Egypt for good as a golden prize.

## History as a Shared Experience

This example also shows us that not only the typical tangled pattern of history, but history itself, is the direct outcome of the constant crossing of the "lives" of the many different societies, for if that was not the case, all histories would be unshared, local ones.

Should all populations had remained stationary, no contact between different groups would have ever been possible. Thus, no mixing of different peoples, no technological or cultural diffusion, no far-reaching explorations or migrations ending in invasions or new settlements, no trade, and also, no competition or clashes between different groups could have ever been observed.

Absence of contact implies too, little or no changes. We can notice this today in the few remaining isolated areas of the world where different peoples live very much by the old customs of their ancestors, either as hunter-gatherers, nomads, herdsmen, primitive peasants, farmers or craftsmen, etc. In such places, one gets the impression history has frozen at various stages, giving us "unspoiled" views of eras we now regard as belonging in the past of humanity.

As the conditions for even relative isolation are rapidly vanishing, we therefore see the extinction of the remaining uncivilized peoples of the world taking place at ever-faster rates. Such groups are either physically destroyed, as their lands are occupied by civilized settlers so that their population dies because of direct killing or relocation to other environments where they are decimated by epidemics, or their cultural identity simply melts away in the civilized sea engulfing them.

Among linguists, it is a familiar fact that the number of dead languages increases every day, so that they have to hurry if wanting to make recordings of the sounds, grammatical structures and semantics of the rapidly vanishing tongues.

On the other hand, the maddening speed of the history of our days is certainly due to more people in more places doing more things, with their comings and goings having an impact or at least a meaning for other people living in the most distant geographies. Rural or isolated areas within developed countries are still regarded as "peaceful," as opposed to the fast pace of life in the big cities, where nothing, including the people in it, seem capable to remain the same.

Now, if the advanced ancient Egypt could not contain the pressure exerted upon it by other peoples, what can we expect from the nations we now regard as world powers?

# 8

# ADVANCED SOCIETIES AND LESS-ADVANCED ONES

## The Demographic Weakness of Developed Nations

We know for sure that today's most advanced nations show a weak or regressive trend in their population growth. The best picture that can be drawn of the contemporary developed countries is one in which ever-increasing living standards correspond to stationary or diminishing populations, especially on the segment of their population that can be called "white" or "national," as opposed to that of the immigrants'.

In fact, according to the most reliable sources[16], without immigration, the population of the most developed areas of the world would start to decline by 2003, shrinking by 126 million by the year 2050. On the year 2000, most countries within Europe, as well as Japan,

Canada, Australia and New Zealand, showed fertility figures below the replacement level (estimated by the United Nations at 2.01 children per woman).

The United States figure for the year 2000 was slightly above the reposition level, probably due to the fertility rates among their non-white population, but because the overall figure is dropping as well, without immigration, its population would equally soon start diminishing.

When taking immigration into consideration, the current projections show that the population of the world's most developed areas will remain roughly the same (meaning the developed countries will be allowing just as many immigrants as needed to keep their numbers constant).

These data confirms all of the population growth of the world coming from within the less-developed areas, and calculations for earlier centuries reveal the exact same pattern, so that we have every reason to think that this is an historical constant, valid too for the ancient past. How can we explain this phenomenon of two apparently opposite demographical behaviors, in function of the degree of development?

## Popular Explanations for Opposed Demographic Behaviors

The most popular explanation for the first behavior proposes that, within rich countries, individuals have become egoists, prone to pleasure, independence and frivolity, thus avoiding marriage. In order to explain the opposite behavior, popular wisdom has it that, in less-developed countries, children are first seen as a source of unpaid work and viewed later as support for the parents as they age. These two explanations could in fact, be reduced to one, as in both cases the pursued goal would be to increase the well being of the grown-ups either by remaining unmarried, or by enhancing their future perspectives through numerous descendants. How much can these views be trusted?

From our hypothetical prehistoric scenario, we left one question behind, namely, that of how each group determines a certain balance between their population numbers and standard of living. We will now retake the issue.

First, we must notice that the original group "A" doubled its size. This means group "A" having a fertility rate which is higher than that of the reposition level, for if that was not the case, their population numbers would have remained constant notwithstanding an extended period of natural abundance encompassing several generations. It is too to be noted that group "A" did not develop a new standard of living. This, because nature did not provide it with any new goods, but rather with just a greater quantity of the same goods already known to them.

It is obvious then, that any group, faced with a greater supply of means of subsistence (as Malthus often called them), will be enabled to grow in numbers. The same effect can be produced, without adding more means of subsistence, if new suitable territories are invaded. Finally, as we have seen, as technology increases production, it facilitates the same outcome. If we were able to invent technology that increased the availability of commodities rather than make new ones (for instance, an irrigation system made possible by the building of a dam), we would observe population growth with a negligible increase in the standard of living.

Now, if this were the only and invariable way human populations could behave, no raising of the living standard would ever have been possible. We must seek therefore, an alternative pattern of behavior. From the observation of primitive groups that have kept their numbers constant through the course of millennia, we can deduce the nature of this alternative behavior.

## Universal Mechanisms Checking Population Growth

Being obvious that primitive groups have too a fertility rate above the reposition level, the only way for them to keep their numbers constant, is to resort to mechanisms that limit reproduction. Even among primitive groups, premarital sex is prohibited and marriages are delayed by social requirements. Hunter-gatherers perform initiation rites that accept a new fellow within the hunter status, thus insuring the new hunter has reached a certain age and gained the ability to support himself and a future family. Within other semi-civilized groups, weddings are the occasion for big ceremonies often involving the whole of the tribes related to the engaged individuals, so we can regard them as expensive, thus limiting their frequency. In some other cases, the groom has to go through a process that starts with the negotiation of a price for the engagement with the family of the bride. He must obtain his own family or tribe's support of the deal, the rearing, harvesting and handcrafting of the agreed goods, plus the erection of a new dwelling for the future wife.

It is evident that groups behaving in this manner are, though unconsciously, preventing their numbers to proliferate over their productive capabilities. Could we consider these tribes being composed too by egoist, pleasure prone individuals? The answer is obviously negative, and so it must be for all the groups descended from them, not mattering how developed they are.

Social mechanisms checking population growth, which I consider universal to all groups, civilized or not, are not merely directed towards protecting their living standard. What is at stake is the very survival of the group, for in the long run, any group not restricting its growth would eventually face disintegration or extinction. The known cases of societies that have collapsed in conditions of relative isolation allow us to say so. Poor or limited lands exploited unwisely led to civilizations that, after experiencing a flourishing period, eventually had to disperse and abandon their best creations, such as cities or temples.

Using the former guidelines, let us try to imagine the probable level of stabilization for a group that, like the "AB," has developed technology. Such group, because of being descended from the "A," has inherited a fertility rate higher than the reposition level. Because of this, and faced with enhanced productive capabilities, it cannot avoid recovering its previous demographic level, and for the very same reason, it cannot avoid keep growing still further. But, should group "AB" stabilize its population precisely at the limit of its productive capabilities, the least unfavorable change in nature would be enough to put it under the direst circumstances. Such a group would be an unstable one, prone to losing population by death or migration, or disintegrating. On the other hand, groups, which unconsciously left an ample margin between their productive capabilities and their population numbers, would be more stable, thus favoring their continuity.

As we can see, not only the societies that we have characterized as advanced but also all groups have to stop the growth of their numbers long before reaching their ultimate productive limit. The simplest social organizations do this in an imperceptible way. The purpose behind strange customs such as all of the men sleeping in the same hut, while the wives stay in their own separate dwellings, or artificially extending the lactating period of the newborns up to four years, must undoubtedly be that of procuring a population equilibrium.

In respect to more advanced and numerous groups, the least we can expect is for them to have inherited the same mechanisms restricting population growth. Thus, the existence, regardless of societies or eras, of complex rules restricting sexual contact, cannot respond to any other purpose. As societies grew in numbers, the most primitive mechanisms became ineffective, therefore explaining the appearance of phenomena such as prostitution, abortion, and the multiplication of techniques to avoid pregnancy. Now, what if all these other measures, operating on top of the existing ones, still proved to be insufficient? In that case, more effective preventive means would have to be implemented.

From the observation of contemporary societies that are experiencing depopulation, we can deduce the nature of this other mechanism. Though a hint on what this mechanism might be has already been provided, we shall go back to review the most simple stabilization mechanisms known to us.

## Stabilization within Primitive Groups

Kenyan paleoanthropologist Richard E. Leakey, while writing about his colleagues' findings regarding the !Kung[17], hunter-gatherers inhabiting the Kalahari Desert, belonging to the San peoples, mentions the operation of a system of nurturing homes (crèche). Because in these tribes breast-feeding is extended up to four years, mothers whose milk has stopped flowing have to regularly meet with other women still breast-feeding their babies. As breast-feeding mothers do not ovulate, Leakey speculates this custom may inhibit too the ovulation of the mothers still presenting their children for regular breast-feeding, though he finally reaches no conclusion. He does, however, state that all contemporary hunter-gatherer peoples, in the world, wait 3 to 4 years between one pregnancy and the next. Other anthropologists note that, when preventive measures fail, the mother of unwanted newborns has to decide for herself whether or not to kill them.

Thus, in what we regard as the most simple human societies, ancient customs limiting the number of births—by spacing them—plus others delaying marriage, are enough to keep their numbers constant indefinitely. (Killing a newborn is probably not a population-growth-control measure, but a way of insuring the viability of the infant currently being reared, as the demands posed by an unexpected newborn could compromise the health of both the mother and the child. Among mammals, a female will leave a newborn to die, taking it away from the rest of the litter, if being sick or too weak.)

Now, the case of the tribesman that has to negotiate an engagement price is somewhat more elaborate. Because this system, on top of checking the number of births of already formed couples by means of different customs, also targets the formation of new couples, it could, at least theoretically, produce an imbalance. Should no agreement between the parties involved be reached, the prospect of remaining single would be an open possibility both for the would-be bride and groom. Nevertheless, the appropriate setting of the prices of the engagements would ensure enough new couples being formed, thus achieving demographic stability.

Therefore, in this case and the ones involving big-scale ceremonies, the marriage, a social event, is indirectly linked to the productive possibilities of the group. This link is more evident and effective when it specifically targets the social (or economic) condition of the would-be spouses. Thus, a woman will limit herself to the few possible grooms compatible with her social condition, and vice versa. Our next concern is the means in which these mechanisms were evolved to a degree of making depopulation possible.

## Malthus' Preventive Check

Let us consider a common example in contemporary societies with surplus economies. Let us think of someone in the need of a car. An individual might have enough money for a new, working and dependable automobile. However, that individual might find that the new car that can be afforded is unsatisfactory, according to his or her expectations in terms of social status. Thus, the only way to make the individuals living in surplus economies to still experience scarcity, is by creating an artificial one by means of devaluing the most common or accessible goods.

The effectiveness of this mechanism is insured (very much as in all of the others), by targeting everyone at a very early age.

So, in today's most advanced societies we observe most individuals of every new generation trying to keep the living standard they have inherited from their parents. In most cases this will mean the individual having to go through a much longer process than in less-developed societies, requiring more years of education, or having accumulated enough wealth in a given trade, or achieved success in an independent profession, etc. As many individuals will have enough trouble just maintaining their current living standard, that will prevent them to consider the prospect of marriage and family.

Once again, it was Malthus who first identified these social requirements for status (his "preventive check" to population growth, identified with *"the difficulties attending the rearing of a family"*), though he mistakenly took them as coming from real scarcities within the economic system:

> "There are some men, even in the highest rank, who are prevented from marrying by the idea of the expenses that they must retrench, and the fancied pleasures that they must deprive themselves of, on the supposition of having a family.
>
> A man of liberal education, but with an income only just sufficient to enable him to associate in the rank of gentlemen, must feel absolutely certain that if he marries and has a family he shall be obliged, if he mixes at all in society, to rank himself with moderate farmers and the lower class of tradesmen.
>
> Two or three steps of descent in society, particularly at this round of the ladder, where education ends and ignorance begins, will not be considered by the generality of people as a fancied and chimerical, but a real and essential evil.

The sons of tradesmen and farmers are exhorted not to marry, and generally find it necessary to pursue this advice till they are settled in some business or farm that may enable them to support a family. These events may not, perhaps, occur till they are far advanced in life. The scarcity of farms is a very general complaint in England. And the competition in every kind of business is so great that it is not possible that all should be successful.

The servants who live in gentlemen's families have restraints that are yet stronger to break through in venturing upon marriage. They possess the necessaries, and even the comforts of life, almost in as great plenty as their masters. Their work is easy and their food luxurious compared with the class of labourers. And their sense of dependence is weakened by the conscious power of changing their masters, if they feel themselves offended. Thus comfortably situated at present, what are their prospects in marrying? Without knowledge or capital, either for business, or farming, and unused and therefore unable, to earn a subsistence by daily labour, their only refuge seems to be a miserable alehouse, which certainly offers no very enchanting prospect of a happy evening to their lives. By much the greater part, therefore, deterred by this uninviting view of their future situation, content themselves with remaining single where they are."[18]

Thus, in more developed societies, people are, though unconsciously, encouraged to pursue goals that in themselves, limit or exclude the chance of marrying and creating a family, with the ultimate purpose of such unconscious conditioning still being the noble one of keeping population numbers constant. As the pursued goals are often identified with the possession of the lesser obtainable goods or positions, is easy to understand why the individuals living within developed societies are often depicted as shallow, egoist, or pleasure-prone.

We can confirm not only this newest mechanism, but of all of the previous ones described, being strictly social in nature. Popular music lyrics often denounce the societal "hypocrisy" entrenched in values that ignore the feelings of the "true love" and prevent the engagement of a man—who is poor, lacking formal education, unemployed, from a lower social status, too young, "future-less," or married, etc.—with a single or married woman.

## Depopulation within Developed Societies

How come this "status" mechanism became so effective as to enable depopulation, a phenomenon that has no equivalent in nature? Rather than viewing this mechanism as a different or special one, we should regard it as one merely more evolved or sophisticated than its predecessors, with depopulation obeying a different reason. Since more populated societies are more at risk of overpopulating than less-populated ones, with the overpopulation risk requiring less time for happening, we can only assume all the population checks in the more populated societies acquired an unidirectional operation. Within much less populated groups, we can assume the regulatory function being precisely that, one that adjusts in either sense so as to produce constant populations. But with a population whose only problem is to overpopulate, the regulatory function lost its two way operation, thus evolving only in the direction of containing growth.

We can envision the action of these social checks as if one where stepping into the brakes of a car going downhill. At the very beginning, the action of the brakes would barely produce a reduction of the speed, but as the brakes continue to do their function, the speed would be diminished more rapidly, eventually stopping the car for good. Now if we assume the "brakes" in a society that has already stopped growing, are still performing their function with undiminished strength, the only possible outcome is depopulation.

Depopulation in turn, when noticed, is seen as a lesser evil. If a nation holding tens or hundreds of millions of inhabitants loses for instance, 0.25 percent of its population yearly, this effect will probably worry no one at first. After 50 years, the accumulated population deficit would be a 12 percent, and after a century, the figure would be a much more significant 22 percent. Nevertheless, when regarding this effect as undesirable, we see today's advanced nations resorting to allow immigration, and we can be sure the same solution was used in ancient times.

Now, if all groups and not just the ones we can think as advanced have to inhibit their population growth, how can we explain an opposite behavior? The answer to this question is that there is no opposite behavior, as all the current developed nations were once less-developed societies themselves. It is evident that the demographic growth of an advanced society will be perceived as weak in comparison to less-advanced groups first benefiting from known technologies.

Once more, one of the best descriptions of how less-advanced peoples react when exposed to new technology, comes from Malthus' "*Essay*":

> "It is said that the passion between the sexes is less ardent among the North American Indians than among any other race of men. Yet…it has been frequently remarked that when an Indian family has taken up its abode near any European settlement and adopted a more easy and civilized mode of life, that one woman has reared five, or six, or more children, though in the savage state it rarely happens that above one or two in a family grow up to maturity."[19]

## A Global Demographic Model—The Technologic-Demographic Transference Effect

Directly from here, we can infer a global demographic mechanic that shows, regardless of historical eras, a) advanced societies that because of their territorial expansion, b) get in touch with less-advanced groups, which, c) because of having been exposed to new technologies, are enabled to grow in numbers before stabilizing themselves.

This effect we shall call the "technologic-demographic transference effect," because it induces both changes within the less-developed or recipient group. This demographic model does not conceive human population dynamics having two entirely different ways of operating, or even two extremes being possible within the same behavior, as again, we must accept today's nations experiencing depopulation, first went through phases of rapid growth. Rather than showing differences in behavior, the proposed mechanism depicts the same behavior recurring at different times for each society. This explains the effect by means of which the "vigor" and "dynamism" of "old" and advanced civilizations appears to be regularly transferred throughout history to "new" emerging societies that seem destined to overtake, and eventually, replace them.

How is it that less-developed countries eventually transform themselves into developed ones, thus reproducing a cycle in which their enhanced productive capabilities gradually shift from promoting population growth to promoting higher living standards (allowing the demographic "brakes" to gradually perform its function successfully)?

From the observation of contemporary advanced civilizations living side by side with less-advanced societies, we can see that the technologies, which are most likely to be first implemented by the less-developed group, are those of the most elemental nature. The acquisition of basic technologies is to be favored over the latest, most sophisticated and expensive technological means in the possession of the neighbor, many of which would seem superfluous.

Now, if we compare the demographic effects of advanced technologies such as say, laser microsurgery, satellite data encoding, and X-ray diffraction, against the development or enhancement of irrigation, road, and electric systems, is easy to see why is it that less-developed countries only seem to be growing in numbers perilously. In fact, they are raising their living standards as well. As the first stages concerning the implementation of the most elemental advancements, which as noted, mainly impact agricultural produce prices and availability, improve sanitary conditions, etc., are completed, successive assimilated technologies result in the production of more elaborate, expensive, industrial or "luxury" items. The introduction of newer and scarcer commodities eventually catches the attention of the public, which develops a taste for them.

For instance, in the absence of available TV sets, people will have little or no reason not to live according to the simplest (or only) way known to them. If no new goods are introduced, the demographic effect of basic technologies will be very much like the one seen in China (and in fact, elsewhere in less-developed countries), where governmental policies had to be established in order to discourage population growth. However, when commodities like black-and-white TV sets, for instance, become affordable for greater segments of the public, what we identified as the "social status" mechanism is enabled to operate, with people trying to get their hands on the more scarce, and yet affordable, items.

If later on, black-and-white TV sets are no longer luxury items but basic commodities, then color TVs or big-screen TVs with higher resolution, as well as many other commodities, take the place of the black-and-white TVs first introduced. So, the race to acquire still more expensive-tagged items is enabled to gain momentum indefinitely.

## Cumulative Pattern of Technology and Standard of Living

We now know that the evolution of living standards follows a similar pattern to that of the upward trend of technology, with true cases of regression being rare. Conditions in which living standards drop below their previous level, that is, because of favoring demographic growth, are most likely to happen (though only for limited periods) under tight competition. Let us suppose two rivaling groups, one of them being sensibly more developed than the other.

Under a probabilistic scheme, any of these two groups could prevail, but given the circumstances, both groups would find themselves in the need of extra hands. As we can infer from many cases throughout prolonged periods in history, the characteristic response on the side of the most developed group, rather than growing in numbers, would be the enhancement of its military machinery.

But even this measure, with a negligible or no demographic effect within the advanced society, could however encourage population growth within other related or neighboring groups, as all the previously idle productive resources would be put to work, thus making more produce accessible to more people. In order to enhance its military capabilities, the most advanced group would require two parallel armies, one proper military, and the other assigned to productive tasks. The military army would be recruited from the less privileged ranks of the advanced society, but as this force could prove insufficient, other recruits coming from related, neighboring or friendly groups would be called too. The conformation of the civilian army would follow a similar pattern. Enslaved individuals or others coming from, or living in, less-developed societies, would be assigned to the rudest productive tasks. Using contemporary economic terminology, we would say that massive hiring took place.

While all this would be happening within the most developed society and its area of influence, the main "strategy" of the less-advanced group would be to further grow in numbers, even if this measure meant temporarily "tightening their belts."

There is no chance, however, to indefinitely lower the living standards of a population without causing it to shrink in numbers. Thus, in the majority of the occasions, the perception of plummeting living standards, within any given society, is only deceiving. Vivid descriptions of the conditions of the workers during the English Industrial Revolution, spread the perception of the workers' situation worsening. More accurate analysis from that era have shown that the workers' harsh living in the crowded factories and suburban areas of the English cities actually represented an improvement over their previous conditions as peasants in rural areas. As an aside, this definitely gives us an idea of how precarious the peasants' living must have been.

## The "Threat" of Less-Developed Nations

This last observation leads us to acknowledge a distinct feature we can see regarding the behavior of the individuals living (or coming from) less-developed countries, as compared to those natural to rich nations.

This feature is the comparative colossal efforts the individuals living in less-developed areas (even within the same country) are willing to endure in order to raise their living standards. An immigrant coming from a less-developed country will work to the limit of his physical and intellectual capabilities, and still feel happy about his enhanced means of subsistence. This attitude will in some cases, irritate nationals who will not accept to make comparable efforts for the same low wages or profits. In most cases, second-generation immigrants will not, however, share the same impetus of their parents, as they will be reared in the new country. Finally, third-generation immigrants, in spite of their alien facial features, will probably be ashamed to speak the language of their grandparents, preferring for all purposes to act and look as nationals.

While this fast evolution is possible for immigrants, the overwhelming majority of the individuals who will never have the chance to emigrate, will still be willing to make the same comparatively disproportionate efforts in their own homelands.

We see this today in the form of investment paradises with abundant, cheap and efficient labor. Not many decades ago, less-developed countries were typically supplying the raw materials the powerful industries demanded in rich countries. Now we notice that besides raw materials, all sorts of finished goods are coming from the same regions. This also means the foreign emplacement of new factories (as well as the shutdown of existing ones), as the industry of the developed areas is migrating in masse to the less-developed nations.

So, when we said that war is just the most visible form of competition between different human societies, that was only appropriate, as commercial competition also "undermines" the "strength" of developed nations, leading to their eventual overtake by less-developed countries. Thus the "real danger" for advanced nations is (and has always been) outside of their national borders, as the "danger" immigrants pose is a much lesser "threat."

Right-wing politicians and unions, usually rivaling in their views, find a common ground in their opposition to open their markets to the invasion of foreign-made commodities, asking for tougher measures to "protect" their economies. But this is only a lost cause, for as stated, no individual natural of a rich country would accept to sell his own efforts so cheaply. Most economists and the public as well, understand and accept that imposing stricter barriers to foreign produce would only make many commodities scarce and unaffordable.

Regardless of eras, much of the well being of power centers has come from taking advantage of the cheap and abundant work coming from less-developed areas. This fact that helps us understand why is it that they dive into decline as the less-developed areas acting as their cheap providers cease to perform such a function. The most obvious of these cases are those of many former colonial powers, in which is easy to see that, upon losing their colonies, both their power status and high living standards took an irreversible blow.

Thus, the previous considerations, expressed in the familiar terms of the economic theory, depict in fact, recurrent historical behaviors. Should we take a look at the social and demographic evolution of the Roman Empire, we would be struck by the same facts, namely, the advancement of the less-developed peoples coexisting with them, both within and outside their imperial borders.

Tenacious and implacable against their enemies, the Romans always had in their army the backbone that sustained them through their direst challenges. In its Republican days, when Rome was a tiny state that fought enemies of its own caliber, Latin families, in addition to losing their sons' useful hands to the army, had to pay for their gear and weaponry. As Roman power extended, Latin population became both insufficient and needed in higher positions. Recruits coming from all over the Empire had to be accepted within the army. For this, the recruits were given besides gear and weapons, training, pay, a share of the spoils, and promotions. By the time the Empire had to fight among other barbarians, the Germanic hordes, slaughtering them by the thousands, practically the entirety of their army, including some of their high-ranking officers, were of all ancestries, except Latin, and so were eventually some of their Emperors too.

For all of their strength and ingenuity, the Romans were not able to contain the barbarian tribes still standing against them, that were seeking, so to speak, their share of the pie, and slowly learned how to gain it, thus leading to the downfall of the Empire. Therefore, both the rise and decline of the Roman Empire can be explained in terms of their comparative position among other peoples that evolved first to their advantage, and later against them.

Likewise, the evolution of today's most-developed economies into less industrial and more "service-oriented, high-tech" economies, an effect that can be seen as a natural (and adequate) "response" to the changes in world economy, is, in fact, the last stage today's most advanced nations will know before being toppled also in the "high-tech" sector by the advancements of some of today's less-developed nations.

To summarize, developed and less-developed societies, are the same societies at different times in history.

# 9

# TODAY'S MOST POPULATED COUNTRIES

Early in his lengthy work, Toynbee mentions the only historical challenge he specifically identifies as Malthusian. According to the historian, between the years 725 and 325 B.C., the numerous city-states of Ancient Greece were *"confronted with the problem of the pressure of population upon the means of subsistence"*[20].

Toynbee notes that Corinth and Chalcis disposed of their surplus population by colonizing agricultural territories overseas. Sparta instead, attacked its neighbors gaining little land at a great expense. Athens specialized its agricultural and manufactured production for export, and adjusted its political institutions in order to give a fair share of power to the new classes emerged from the economic transformation. Now, what of the former responses could help China and India out of their present condition?

These two countries have a history far exceeding that of the Ancient Rome. In both cases civilizations within their territories sprang about two millennia B.C. (with the dates for India being somewhat earlier), and because of the size and fertility of their territories, they have been populous since ancient times. Today's enlarged borders of the People's Republic of China cover about the same area as the United States, and India is roughly a third of that. But the most impressive figures about these countries, are the size and low living standards of their populations. China has 1.2 billion inhabitants, and India 1 billion, the two countries together representing slightly more than one third of the world population. Their annual income per capita is a fraction of that of the United States. Depending on what accounting method is used, the figures could be as low as 2.5 and 1.4 percent, or as high as 11.6 and 7 percent, for China and India, respectively.

What was that happened to these two early successful civilizations?

## The Reasons behind the Apparent Backwardness of China and India

An insight to their relative decline is provided by the historian Paul Kennedy in his book *"The Rise and Fall of Great Powers."* According to the historian, by the year 1500, the civilized powers of the world, sharing a comparable degree of development among them, were: 1) The Ottoman Empire, encompassing today's Turkey, Cyprus, Syria, Iraq, Lebanon, Israel, Jordan, Greece, Albania, Yugoslavia, Croatia, Slovenia, Bosnia, Macedonia, Rumania, Bulgaria, and most of Hungary; in northern Africa, it held the northern lands of today's Algeria, Tunisia, Libya and Egypt, and also occupied the west coast of the Arabic Peninsula, 2) The Persian Empire, located in today's Iran, and most of the Arabic Peninsula, 3) The Ming Empire, in most of today's China and Korea, except for the Tibetan plateau, 4) The Mogul Empire, emplaced in today's northern India and Nepal, 5) Muscovy, in today's European Russia and, 6) the nations of Western Europe.

When checking this distribution on a map, one will see the isolation of three of these centers: China, India and Muscovy had no borders with the other powers. The remaining three lived in close contact, fighting regularly between them. Europe was practically surrounded by the Ottoman Empire, while the Ottomans were also sharing borders with the Persian Empire.

The behavior of these powers was as follows: China (and Japan) were accessible—and could reach the rest of the world—by sea. Kennedy reports the Ming navy as having, by the year 1420, 1350 combat vessels, including 400 large floating fortresses and 250 ships designed for long-range cruising. By 1436, however, an imperial edict banned the construction of sea-going ships and later, ships with more than two masts were too forbidden. Japan soon followed China self-containment policies, restricting their own ventures overseas. The Mogul Empire was, according to Kennedy, even more inward-oriented than Ming China, their imports being only luxury items. Muscovy, though without borders with Western Europe, imported many of their developments. The Ottoman Empire was pushing against Europe, putting Vienna under siege in two occasions, and would eventually defeat the Persian Empire.

In regards to the nations of Europe, Kennedy notes that they were the only civilized powers not being a centralized Empire. Besides fighting the Turks (and sometimes using them as allies), they had the added weight of competing with each other, with no single nation or block being able to subdue the others for good. First, the Spanish, holding the thrones of Castile, Aragon, the Netherlands, Austria, Sicily, Naples and Burgundy, attempted to control the rest of the continent, to no avail. Later on, France's try to reign over all of Europe was checked by the English, Prussian, Austrian, and Russian. Finally, well into the 20th century, the Germans would make the last effort to achieve pan-European domination.

Thus, it was within the politically diverse Europe that a dynamic, driven by economical and technological advances, evolved at such an accelerate rate that would eventually more than compensate Europe's relative demographic weakness in their latter quest for world domination. (Kennedy mentions China having by the 15th century between 100 and 130 million inhabitants, versus 50 to 55 million for Europe.) Then, if the dynamism of Europe was a direct consequence of prolonged competition, the self-containment of the Chinese and Mogul empires would explain their relative decay.

But, what in turn explains the self-containment policies of these empires? Were they not already isolated?

The Chinese quitting their sea expeditions and letting their formidable navy to rot, and the fact that the Mogul Empire imported only luxury goods, are clear indications of how much these empires lacked the need of the external word. Their "self-containment" is then, much better understood in terms of self-sufficiency, the external world representing only a source for possible trouble (in modern times, isolationism also sprang within the United States).

Kennedy notes the openness of the European countries of that time by pointing out that the trade within them was of bulk products such as timber, grain, wine, wool, herrings and so on. But we have every reason to believe that traffic of this nature existed also within the Ming and the Mogul Empires, the only difference being that they did not need to trade with foreign parties.

Kennedy also mentions the fact of China's iron furnaces producing 125,000 tons per annum (mainly for the military) at the end of the 11th century, a greater output than that of England at the beginning of the Industrial Revolution, seven centuries later. By the year 1736, however, the blast furnaces and coke ovens of Honan and Hopei were abandoned, and they would not resume operation until the 20th century.

This last "strange," fact should illustrate us on how large the surplus of iron, by Chinese standards, must have been by 1736. So to speak, the worlds of the Chinese and Mogul Empires, were completely "done," lacking nothing they regarded as useful. Thus the apparent "backwardness" of China and India are obvious only in retrospective, and the same can be said about the European "dynamism." Just like the existence of unfulfilled needs determines the production of new developments, their absence determines just the opposite.

Therefore, it was indeed due to their needs, that the nations of Western Europe were to colonize the entirety of the American continent, and large parts of the African. Kennedy cites the Chinese navy of admiral Cheng Ho that reached Africa between the years 1405 and 1433, as being able to "discover" Portugal decades before Henry the Navigator's own navy ventured too into Africa. But this only tells us Henry the Navigator had reasons to pay for an expensive expeditionary navy, while the Chinese had powerful reasons not to invest further on their own. (The Great Wall, designed to contain the Mongols, was constructed not much later by the same Ming Dynasty.) In very much the same way, some 500 years before Columbus, the Viking nobleman Leif Ericson set foot on Canada, where archeological remains of a Viking settlement have been identified at Newfoundland. So, just as Columbus, Ericson also had the means to reach American shores, being any significant need to colonize, what both the "aborted" Viking civilization, and the Ming empire, lacked entirely.

At this point, the reasons why today's China and India are the most populated countries in the world, while also belonging to the list of today's less-developed nations, should be no mystery. In earlier pages we said that if Egypt had remained isolated, it would exist still today, virtually unchanged. Then, even assuming some degree of change during the course of three millennia for our supposed "preserved contemporary Egyptian society," how high would their standard of living be? In spite of any improvements such a society could have produced on its own, their current income, measured in economic terms, would be a dismally small figure, just like the ones of China and India.

Now, having been populous since ancient times, we should expect China and India remaining at least as populous as they used to be, unless their soils were unwisely exploited. (Though Egypt's area is about a third of India, their 64 million people have to live in the 10 percent of their territory not covered by the desert). Therefore, China and India's populations, in absence of contact with new technology, should had remained either stable or varying (increasing or decreasing) at a very slow pace. But, as both China and India were stung by European powers in the 18th century, and from our proposed global demographic model, we can infer these countries have suffered since then, from the "technologic-demographic transference effect."

## Demographic Explosions in Historic Times

Our global demographic model, in effect, proposes that when less-developed groups assimilate technology, the first symptom they show is an increase of their population. Should we take a look at a world population graphic in historic times, we would be able to identify at least three demographic explosions. After the Neolithic Revolution—the transition period when many human groups gave up hunting and gathering to agriculture—the first steep increase of population happened after the year 2000 B.C. Although the first agricultural practices date back as early as 10,000 B.C., no metal technology was available at that time. Bronze, iron, ox-drawn plows, and other developments such as grain storage came much later, being common to many societies around the year 2000 B.C. A second inflection point on the curve of human population occurred after 1750, as the developments of the Industrial Revolution were first produced in England, and later, spread to other areas of the world. The third and more marked inflection point on the curve of demographic growth of humanity, happened after 1950, thanks to the forced contact of many previously isolated regions with the most advanced societies of that time, all this, because of the world mobilization provoked by the Second World War.

As we can see, population explosions occur only after the development of powerful new technology (it could not be otherwise), with the better part of them, if not the explosions themselves, happening only when the more advanced technology "hits" less-developed societies.

Then, the recent, explosive growth of the populations of China and India is the direct effect of these societies having being exposed to more powerful technologies developed elsewhere. But as we know, this is only the first stage of a process that has repeated itself in countless occasions throughout history. After an initial stage of steep population growth, consecutive slowdowns in the rate of population growth should be observed, along with more significant improvements in the standard of living, all this, finally leading to the stabilization and possible decrease of the populations involved.

As an outcome of this process, there is also the possibility of the development of new technologies leading to the appearance of previously unknown ways of life.

But, why should we contemplate this possibility?

This question is only pertinent. Today's second world economic power, Japan, did not develop any new technological means leading to the appearance of a new way of life. In fact, the ingenuity of the Japanese people has been repeatedly questioned by Western opinions. According to such views, the Japanese can only replicate whatever it has been done by other developed countries (though rarely mentioning that such Japanese "copies" are usually much better and cheaper). Why then, did not the Japanese develop new technologies on their way up?

It is very clear that neither Japan, nor Germany—the two main losers of the Second World War—because of the size of their populations, were in the need of producing unknown technological means. After their defeat, both nations did their best not only to rebuild themselves, but also to become (or reaffirm as) economic powers, being able to surpass the United States in terms of per capita income. What does this last fact mean?

For developed countries with small populations (or scarcely populated nations with enormous natural resources like oil), it is relatively easy to surpass the per capita income figure of the United States. We can cite as examples Luxembourg (having less than half a million inhabitants), Liechtenstein (with a population less than 50,000), and occasionally (depending on what method is used), Switzerland (7.2 million), or Norway (4.4 million). But it is no small feat for a "standard" developed country to surpass the United States economic performance. Both Japan, with a population somewhat less than a half of the United States, and Germany, with a population somewhat less than a third of the United States, were able to accomplish such a achievement in postwar times.

This extraordinary outcome reveals the need of the Japanese and German peoples to recover their national pride, badly hurt after their military defeat. On the other hand, Russia maintained a virtual state of war not only with the United States (though mainly against them), but also with the rest of the developed nations of the world. Because of their economical weaknesses, the Soviets were not able to compete civilly, so they turned to military competition, replicating, and sometimes even taking the lead in such technological races as the nuclear and space exploration. These facts, in turn, reveal the enormous need of the Soviets to equate themselves with the United States as a world power.

Today, the more-normal economic performances of Japan and Germany (although still very good, as they are indisputably the second and third economic world powers) and the changed political status within Russia leave the United States as the world leader in terms of economic and military strength. (Today's Russian Federation, in its dire economic condition, is down to the tenth economy of world, falling behind those of China, India, France, the United Kingdom, Italy and Brazil.)

## China and India's Imminent Transformation

Now we must ask, *Will China and India ever catch up to the United States' standard of living? And if so, will these countries find, just as Japan and Germany did, enough power in the existing technologies to satisfy the needs of their population?* The following example depicts the situation.

If, by miracle, China and India were to reach the United States' standard of living, say, by tomorrow, China and India would be economic powers about 4.5, and 3.6 times, respectively, that of the United States. Translated in terms of existing technologies, this would mean reproducing some eight times the United States' basic infrastructures. These include road, energy and communication systems, industrial and transportation means, as well as civil facilities such as housing, offices, schools, restaurants, cinemas, hotels, supermarkets, stadiums, etc. This task would imply more than duplicating the size of the world's economy. Could this feat be done?

Assuming spectacular rates of economic growth, such as 10 percent yearly, these countries would reach their goal within 50 years, a time when, presumably, the United States would be much more advanced than today. Assuming more believable rates of growth such as 5 percent a year, the task of meeting the living standards of today's United States, would take them a little less than a century. What this exercise suggests, is that in spite of any achievements, neither China nor India would ever reach the living standard of the United States.

Both countries would be condemned of advancing towards a goal like Achilles and the Tortoise in Zeno of Elea's famous paradox. (Remember Achilles, a swift runner that never caught up with a tortoise moving ahead of him? When Achilles reached the first juncture, where the tortoise was, the tortoise had already moved, and so on.) The countries would get closer with each step, but never actually getting there.

We had to wait some 2,500 years for anybody to provide a solution for Zeno of Elea's paradox of Achilles and the Tortoise. German mathematician Georg Cantor's solution basically states that the sum of an infinite series such as $1+1/2+1/4+1/8+...+1/n$, has a finite value, meaning Achilles finally catches up with the tortoise. In a similar way, nevertheless experience tells us less-developed countries do catch up and even surpass more advanced ones, it is far from obvious how this process happens. Let us see in more detail our past assumptions using a more concrete example.

Suppose China and India both decide to launch in 2005, an ambitious 20-year program to meet the international advanced standard say, in telephony, to service most of their populations. So they start to lay the telephone poles and suspend the wiring needed, and go on building all the telephonic exchange centers required, etc., until they successfully reach the (initial) advanced standard, right on schedule. But by 2025, both countries would find, very much to their surprise, that they are still behind the international advanced standard, because during the 20 years their programs lasted, new developments were produced. So, by 2025, both China and India decide to launch a second program, this time to catch up with the 2025 standards, by the year 2035. When both countries successfully reach the 2025 standards by 2035, again, they would have to recognize their systems still being a decade behind of that of the advanced standard, and so on. This is, as we have seen, the "Zeno of Elea" approach to the problem. Is there a way out of the paradox (and depict what really happens)?

Let us suppose that after a decade of the launching of China and India's first telephonic program, both countries switch to an all-satellite operated system, thus catching up, and maybe even surpassing Western standards.

Now, even accepting such a system as a feasible one, why would China and India be the first countries to develop it? Would it not be more likely instead that today's most advanced nations were first in producing such a technology? We will now explore this other possibility. To start with, why would any advanced countries develop this new system?

Unless they found out that, because of the new system being sensibly more cost-effective, any investments would be profitable within a reasonable period, such a project would never take place. For the sake of the example, let us suppose that such a system is both economically and technologically viable, so that it is developed. How long would it take for China and India to follow? Could not they be stuck with the pole- and wire technology for decades?

These countries would soon be forced to switch to the new satellite-based system. Otherwise, going ahead with their programs with an obsolete technology would mean to invest twice to solve the same problem, as they would be faced immediately (or before) completing their infrastructure, with the need of replacing it anew. In other words, China and India will restore as soon as they can, to any new technology promising to solve their needs for good. Meanwhile, the newly finished Western system would not be replaced for a long time because the number of real users (people) would remain roughly the same.

Now, what if such a project though technologically feasible, turned not to be profitable within developed countries (meaning their existing installations and technologies had still a long life ahead of them)? In that case, the first countries to develop such a technology would be indeed China and India. Aware of the same fact—the technical feasibility of such a powerful system—China and India would not weigh the same issue on the Western terms. Because for the better part of their users they would not be replacing any old systems, but providing the service for the very first time, the profitability of investing in the new technology would actually be higher for them. In fact, such a technology would find its widest application and eventual refinement, within China and India, regardless of who the original developers could be.

If we take a look at today's developed nations, we will notice that the needs of most of their populations are adequately satisfied. Although new homes, bridges, airports, roads, hospitals, schools, etc., are being built within developed countries, the rate at which this replacement or enlargement of their existing facilities is done is a very slow one. If measured in economic terms, the rate would translate to almost zero growth (if counting depreciation as a factor). So to speak, the better part of their economic infrastructures is very much done, thus leaving little room for improvement.

These countries still manage to report a steady economic growth, however, because technological advancements induce two effects into their economies, the first one, being that of obsolescence. As improvements in technology often translate into bettered goods, the populations within these countries are driven to replace their "old" commodities for the newer versions of them. Technology also adds strictly new goods and services on top of the existing ones. Microcomputers, cell phones, and medical breakthroughs are good examples, though there are many cases in which clearly differentiating between new goods or merely bettered ones, will prove to be a hard exercise (such as in videotape players versus DVD's).

Anyway, it is in this narrow field of technological progress that the economies of advanced countries still manage to grow at rates that fall typically between 1 and 2 percent a year. By contrast, less-developed countries can show growth rates peaking at 10 percent in a year, easily averaging 5 percent in longer periods. Now, the arithmetical difference between these figures entails that less-developed countries do catch up. Eventually, as less-developed countries gradually transform themselves into more advanced ones (like Japan), their rate of economic growth also shows a decline. Otherwise, rather than catching up, these countries would surpass any advanced standards.

This later possibility will eventually happen in the case of China and India.

Since the size of their unfulfilled needs is enormous, China and India's economies will behave (or are already doing so) very much like a car speeding downhill, its only brakes being that of the car's own inertia. Supposing the hill having a moderate but constant inclination, at first, the car would start to move slowly, but as the car's inertia gives way to the gravitational force, the car will accelerate at a steady rate, stopping its race only long after the hill has leveled. Taking the size of the unfulfilled needs as the hill's inclination, we would have to say that the Western hill is almost flat. The steep hills facing China and India will allow them, as they race to meet Western's living standards, to reach the finish line by halfway down the hill. In other words, their standard of living would stabilize not in function of having reached any initial goal they had as a reference, but only in accordance to the level represented by the possibilities of their new technological means.

Thus, the reason behind the technological "weakness" of many developed societies of all times, has been their lack of need. Constant populations, even taking into account—or perhaps because of—immigration, have found themselves adequately serviced by their existing infrastructures, thus, creating a condition in which, in spite of their technological advancement, developed societies did not find any suitable fields for further expansion, as seen in the case of the Greco-Roman world.

We have invoked the same reasons to explain the effects of war over technology. For an advanced society that otherwise would not experience new or stronger needs, the event of war operates as a challenge that thrusts both its ingenuity and economy. The First World War pressed the United States' economy with extraordinary demands. As Europe was in war, grain and many other commodities, and eventually, military force, were sent to the European allies (the peace being the reason behind the Great Depression). Again, the Second World War was the reason behind the amazing breakthroughs that revolutionized the whole of the United States' industry and economy, as a result of which, this country alone ended being responsible for about 50 percent of the world's economic output.

So, even if China and India apparently have no choice but to improve their economies resorting to existing technologies, because of the unparalleled size of their unfulfilled needs, will bear a constant pressure to rely on ever more powerful technologies. Furthermore, as the most advanced technological means (and the resources exploited by them) in use in contemporary advanced societies, are already "obsolete" to meet China and India's demands, the better part of these countries' now inexistent infrastructures, when finished, will resemble nothing we now know.

Emerging countries have always as an initial reference, the most advanced technological means of the neighbor, and by this stage of our technologic-demographic expansive process, it is evident that the United States and Canada, the European Union, Japan and Australia, are already "neighbors" of China and India. In the same fashion, the goal of the populations of emerging countries is to obtain for themselves the same standard of living the most advanced neighbor enjoys.

Now, imagine China and India trying to meet the living standards of today's most advanced countries by reproducing only their known technologies. Throughout all of recorded history, living standards have been raised because of cities. Cities are the centers where most commodities are produced and consumed, the wealth of any developed nations being heavily concentrated in them. Not surprisingly, all of today's advanced countries have managed their transformation from mainly rural countries, to mainly urban ones. In the United States, the population in rural areas is around 3 percent of their total, and similar proportions can be observed for all developed nations. But in the cases of China and India, nearly 70 percent of their populations live in their rural areas. Should they try to follow the same pattern of development all the advanced countries have, China and India would have to build cities large enough to house about 1.5 billion people.

Since today's largest cities hold about 20 to 30 million inhabitants, and, setting this figure at the average of 25 million, China and India would have to build roughly 60 new urban areas of that size. The population living in those cities would be larger than that of all of today's developed countries together.

If we now take into consideration the use an average urban citizen of a developed country makes of such basic resources as water and energy, then we know this feat could not be done. More than one Earth would be needed to provide for these resources (thus explaining the concern of today's developed nations over the ongoing industrialization of the less-developed world).

The future scenario of developed nations competing for prolonged periods over natural resources (such as water), against emerging countries, is, however, unlikely. This assumption implies technology to stagnate at its present level, while our capabilities for technological development, at least for the moment, have no known limits.

So, the reasons behind our present technologies being "resource-intensive," and thus "inefficient" and environmentally disruptive, are utterly simple.

As stated, the goal of technology is to produce a desired effect, which means the first technology proving good enough to deliver the desired effect, being put to use, as any efforts towards exceeding the desired effect would be pointless. Abiding also by the terms of our definition of technology as "all means used by man to modify nature for his advantage of purposes," we should note that all technology had to be more or less disruptive to the environment. This holds true because even prehistoric hunter-gatherers collecting flint stone to make their arrowheads, or adzes (tools employed to work wood), had to disturb nature as it was. Finally, since as recently as 1960, we were half the population we are now, we have not been developing less-disruptive technologies for long enough (environmental concern is too a relatively new phenomena, as Greenpeace was founded in 1971).

Concern alone will not, however, lead us to more powerful (and cleaner) technologies, as concern, compared to necessity, is a much weaker force. So, it will be the countries trying to increase their low living standards under an condition of scarcity of the traditional resources, who will eventually produce the more effective technologies of tomorrow that, because of not relying on any scarce natural resources, will be zero-environmentally-disruptive.

If we want to envision what these future technologies might look like, an easy way to do it is to identify whatever inefficiencies our present technologies have. For the sake of exemplifying, let us think of homes. Even the best of today's homes, besides being very expensive, require a good deal of maintenance, can catch fire, get infested by all sorts of plagues, be destroyed by floods, earthquakes or hurricanes, etc., not to mention the size of the energy bills they generate. An ideal future home would then be one that could take care of its own maintenance, be immune to fires, plagues, floods, earthquakes, etc., produce its own energy, remain communicated at all times. In addition, the place would take care of the dweller's needs such as potable water, food, communications, entertainment, medical supervision, etc.

It is very likely too, that future technologies will not make use of any heavy infrastructures or massive production and distribution facilities, meaning their effects could be reproduced anywhere, such as in the middle of—an otherwise unpopulated—desert. Some of these technologies are already known, though still on their infancies, such as photovoltaic and thermal solar energies, as well as that coming from the wind, or sea tides. New materials that are lighter, more lasting, require less maintenance, and could even be "intelligent" if combined with sensors and computer technologies, that today are inexistent or too expensive to replace the ordinary ones, seem, nevertheless, to be the only alternative in the future. For the purposes of obtaining power, the reaction of hydrogen with oxygen much more energetic than that of burning gasoline. All these technological means are scarcely used today because the needs or applications they would target are all well covered by the current means.

When the technologies that now are considered as "alternative"—as well as others that today exist only in theory—get fully developed, becoming mainstream applications, the roles between today's advanced nations, and countries like China and India will have been reversed. Not only "old style" homes will get more expensive to be built and maintained, but so will be all other structures needed or produced by our present technologies, causing millions of tons of modern infrastructure to become as obsolete as the Pyramids of Egypt.

# PART THREE

# THE HISTORY OF THE FUTURE

# 10

# THE TECHNOLOGY OF THE FUTURE

Russian scientist Konstantin E. Tsiolkovsky (author of *"A Rocket into Cosmic Space,"* published in 1903) and American engineer Robert H. Goddard (who wrote *"A Method of Reaching Extreme Altitudes,"* published in 1919) during the 1920s agreed that it was possible to build liquid-fuel rockets that could reach the Moon, and almost no one believed them. Today, another proposal regarding a technology of the future is currently debated among scientists, and just like in the 1920s, no one knows what the outcome will be.

## Feynman's Talk—Drexler's Approach

The first precedent of this technology was outlined by American Nobel laureate physicist Richard P. Feynman, in a 1959 talk before the American Physical Society at the California Institute of Technology (Caltech). Though Feynman's issue, miniaturization, was hardly a new one, the scale involved was enough to astonish anyone. After pondering such things as why we cannot write the entire 24 volumes of the

Encyclopedia Brittanica on the head of a pin (concluding we can), Feynman stated: "The principles of physics, as far as I can see, do not speak against the possibility of maneuvering things atom by atom. It is not an attempt to violate any laws; it is something, in principle, that can be done; but in practice, it has not been done because we are too big," and the outcome of working at such level would be "to synthesize absolutely anything."[21]

Decades after Feynman's talk, another American researcher, unaware of Feynman's proposals, was developing his own approach to a molecular technology. The researcher was also inspired by Feynman's source of interest, namely, biological phenomena happening in the minute inners of the cell where proteins, the building blocks of a living organism, are synthesized. In his book *"Engines of Creation,"* published in 1986, K. Eric Drexler, described the possibilities of a technology that would work by assembling any structures molecule by molecule (rather than atom by atom). To give us an idea of the scale involved, the widely used prefix "micro," belonging to the metric system, refers to something which is 1000 times smaller than the unit, thus, a millimeter being 1000 times smaller than the meter, the standard metrical unit of length. A microprocessor, so called because it performs the function of thousands (and now, even millions) of transistors, most of the times, is still visible to the human eye. The prefix "nano," used to describe things 1000 times smaller than the micro level—one million times smaller than the unit—was the one chosen by Drexler to name his version of a molecular technology, and so the term "nanotechnology" was coined.

By 1976, Drexler was considering the possibilities if one could design and build molecular robots, as geneticists were already working within the cell. (In fact, by 1982, the United States had approved the medical use of insulin produced by recombinant DNA. By isolating the human gene—a large string of molecules—responsible for the production of insulin, and inserting it into the DNA of the bacteria Escherichia Coli, a previously unimaginable supply of insulin, until then obtained from grinded pork pancreases, was made available.)

Molecular robots, Drexler thought, could handle individual molecules, thus assembling directly any structures, a practice that would leave chemical synthesis 100 percent obsolete. Because everything in the material world is made out of atoms, nanotechnology would not be simply a technology of the future, but rather, the technology of the future. Using molecular technology, scientists could synthesize any object; its complexity does not matter. For instance, Chapter 4 of Drexler's book describes the process of production of a rocket engine that, because of not having been touched by anything larger than a bacteria, would be a solid object in one piece. The rocket engine would lack such inner weaknesses as welding joints, and also would be 90 percent lighter, as all redundant mass not performing any structural function would be eliminated, therefore, making the engine more reliable and efficient.

But the applications of Drexler's nanotechnology defy the imagination. Because the most complex structures in the universe, namely living organisms, are also made by molecules, nanomachines would be able to penetrate a human body to perform any kind of maintenance. This field of nanotechnology was already called "cell repair technology," because it would work within the cells themselves.

The nanomachines described by Drexler are of three kinds: assemblers, replicators, and nanocomputers.

Because proteins cease to work when fried, dried or frozen, a first generation of protein assemblers would be needed to produce a second, much tougher generation that would not share the weaknesses of biomolecules, thus, resisting acids, as well as high pressures and extreme temperatures.

The assembler is the basic nanomachine. Similar to DNA in size and functions, it would be, however, much more versatile. DNA directs all molecular processes within the cell, though never leaving its nucleus.

DNA relies instead, on three types of RNA to perform the work outside the nucleus. One type, the messenger RNA (mRNA), carries the instructions for protein synthesis, the transfer RNA (tRNA), takes the proper amino acids to be processed to the ribosomes (the protein factories of the cell), where the ribosomal RNA (rRNA), performs the synthesis. Assemblers could take care of both the functions of DNA and RNA, and also those of enzymes (large proteins acting as catalysts).

Like DNA, assemblers could perform the feat of reproducing themselves, in which case the assembler is called a replicator. Like a controlled virus, replicators would copy themselves a certain number of times, and then be reprogrammed to perform whatever other functions needed.

Finally, nanocomputers, computers as powerful as the most powerful ones we know today, but built to the scale of bacteria, would provide all instructions, telling the army of assemblers what to do.

The combined powers of this technology would be as much as this: One assembler, programmed to replicate itself at a rate of a million atoms per second, would take a thousand seconds, that is, fifteen minutes, the time it takes a bacteria to reproduce, to create its first copy. After a little more than a day, the replicator would have reached the mass of the Sun and its Planets together.

Nanotechnologic processes therefore, would have to be strictly controlled. In a first stage, a replicator placed in a proper environment would copy itself a certain number of times. On a second stage, the resulting army of assemblers would be directed to perform different tasks. Once the processes are finished, the assemblers and nanocomputers would be discarded, recovered, destroyed or integrated to the finished structure. If adequately used, nanothechnology presumably would solve any poverty problems, allowing humans lots of leisure time, avoiding too all kinds of illnesses, and even death.

## Dangers of a Molecular Technology

Any technology, however, the more powerful, the more potentially destructive. At least until now, the three rules I can think as applicable for all any technologies, are: 1) if they are feasible, they are eventually developed, 2) there is no way to keep them only in "good hands" or direct them exclusively towards "constructive" ends, 3) there is no way for the original developers of a new technology to avoid its replication by other groups or societies.

Let us think of aviation. Rule number one tells us that only its physical impossibility would have prevented the development of aircrafts. Rule number two means that if planes could be used for dropping bombs in war, spying, or illegal trafficking, etc., they would be used for those purposes too. Finally, rule number three tells us the original development of the Wright brothers would be replicated many times. In fact, in its initial stage, because of the First World War, aviation was to be developed more rapidly by European countries. Therefore, the mere idea that any technologies can be controlled or put to use only for pacific or "good" uses, is ridiculous, this, not because of any defect of the technologies themselves, but rather, because of the many flaws of human societies.

Using again our three rules, we have then that, 1) if nanotechnology is feasible, it will be developed, 2) there is no safe way to control its applications, and 3) there is no way to tell who will first develop it, and in any case, once developed it will be reproduced by any parties interested in it.

# 11
# APPROACHING THE NATURAL LIMITS

Drexler and Feynman's proposals reflect how close we are to reach the limits of the physically feasible. Should we expect Drexler's nanotechnology being developed say, within a few decades? Critics of Drexler's nanotechnology have pointed out that no molecular machines have yet been developed in laboratories (though artificial molecular structures have). They have stated that even if molecular robots were developed, they probably would lack, unlike DNA, the ability to replicate themselves. Critics have said also that there is no way to assure molecular machines could be able to identify the correct position of atoms and molecules within other structures, a feat that they would have to perform since millions of such machines would have to work coordinately under zero tolerance for mistakes. Finally, doubts have been expressed on what the source of energy of nanomachines would be once working deep in the intricacy of molecular environments.

Yet, the underlying principle in Drexler's proposal could not be simpler. Replicating nature's workings is an idea so old, that agriculture itself arose out of mimicking nature's processes. In fact, and as stated, the essence of technology is that of modifying nature so as to produce a desired effect.

So, even if Drexler's approach to a molecular technology proves to be flawed, we should bear no doubts about a growing number of attempts to manipulate nature's most basic building blocks, atoms and molecules, being actively researched in many laboratories throughout the world. The least we should expect from such efforts is the price of most known goods and services dropping in astonishing proportions, as well as the appearance of new materials and techniques capable of achieving previously unimaginable tasks (such as producing unlimited amounts of human insulin out of bacteria).

Now, what if Drexler's proposals are fully developed? Then, just as Tsiolkovsky and Goddard envisioned liquid-fuel rockets reaching the Moon some four decades before it actually happened, we should expect seeing nanotechnology performing every feat we have been told it will be able to do.

## A Limit Technology—Inexhaustible Natural Resources—A Fixed Standard of Living

For our purposes, let us call a fully developed molecular technology—Drexlerian or not—a "limit technology," not only because it would be working on the very limits of the physically feasible, but also because it presumably could not be replaced by another yet more powerful.

The last statement implies that such a technology would make the multiplying value of all technologies a constant one. In fact, a "limit technology" would probably induce the same effect on the value of our variables, natural resources and standard of living. Because all natural resources can be expressed in terms of matter, space and energy, and, assuming the quantities of matter, space and energy existing in the universe remaining roughly the same as they are today, a "limit technology" would cause natural resources to assume also a constant value. As for the standard of living, if we accept our population will stabilize as predicted, under a constant, though powerful technology using inexhaustible natural resources, its value would also remain fixed.

What does the previous mean?

Stable indicators for all the four of our variables, imply a stable way of living. Such a way of living could last, just as humanity's hunter-gatherer stage, unchanged for millions of years, and would diverge in character no less from our present, civilized way of living. Before trying to imagine how we evolved from a civilized way of life to a post-civilized one or what a post-civilized way of live would look like, we will review our past assumptions in terms of the economic theory.

The following premises are implied in every economic theory: 1) resources are scarce, 2) needs are preexisting and can only increase, and, 3) the goal of the economic system is to coordinate the adequate production and distribution of goods and services among the individuals immersed in the economic environment.

As the resources exploited by a "limit technology" would be the same atoms over and over, its energy coming from the most abundant source known, namely, that of the Sun, the first economic assumption, that of scarcity, would vanish. Though we are rarely aware of it, all natural resources acquire they usefulness, and thus become scarce, because of the technologies in use. Flint stone was a very important natural resource during prehistoric times, but flint stone is now irrelevant as a source of wealth. Similarly, petroleum, a very important natural resource in these times, had no impact in the lives of the subjects of the Roman Empire, and so did uranium during the times of the British Empire.

Thus, it is the technology in use what determines which aspects of the nature are regarded as "resources." One day we might run out of petroleum, but we will never run out of hydrogen, because besides being the most common form of matter in the universe, in most practical cases hydrogen remains unchanged. Hydrogen can be transformed into a different kind of atoms through fusion, releasing great amounts of energy in this process, which is why the Sun is always giving off energy. But as the most common reactions occurring on the surface of the Earth are chemical, the atoms themselves never undergo any nuclear transformations. Thus, a "limit technology," on top of making natural resources inexhaustible, would relieve us from cutting any trees, mining any ores, or building gigantic dams.

The second economic premise, that of preexisting and ever-increasing needs would collapse too. In these times, for most demands to be fulfilled for the final consumer, there is a waiting period that has nothing to do with the relative scarcity or abundance within a given economy. Except for cases where our demands are instantly met such as turning on the lights or getting tap water, most goods or services even if readily available at a marketplace have to be retrieved, contracted, bought, transported or delivered. And in the case of the ingredients of a regular meal, they may require further processing. A "limit technology," because of working at speeds that defy our imagination (a million atoms per second or one atom per nanosecond), and because of the probable size of its facilities (the core of them being not larger than a thimble), would probably satisfy almost any need upon demand. Delivery would occur without the need to wait or move.

Finally, because of what we have just said, the third economic premise, that of the need to coordinate the production and distribution of goods and services among the individuals belonging to any given economy, would collapse too. This, providing everyone had an equal access to the "limit technology."

## Social Limitations and other Objections

This last supposition leads us to a series of objections to our previous conclusion about reaching a stable way of life.

First, what would guarantee all individuals having an equal access to the possibilities of a "limit technology?" Could it not be the privilege of wealthy individuals or corporations, or, for security reasons, be retained under the control of national governments? Could it not happen that future societies be split into two isolated sectors, those of the "haves" and the "have-nots?" Besides, a "limit technology" as described, would not have per se, the capability to provide us with time travel. If time travel now seems like a bizarre necessity, let us note that just a few decades ago the need for anyone to own a personal computer would have been incomprehensible. Even for stationary populations, should their needs continue to grow indefinitely, a condition of "unlimited resources" would never be reached. By some accounts, time travel is possible (space-time travel, actually), but only by spending enormous quantities of energy. So if desiring time travel, we could exhaust all of our planetary sources of energy, then that of the Sun, and later on, we would have to move out even of our own galaxy, in the search for more vast supplies of energy.

Do we have a way out of these objections? Up to this point, the answer is a negative one. Throughout these pages, we have neglected a couple of analysis that would provide us with definitive information. The first has to do with the internal structure of human societies. So far, we have directed our attention to describe and explore the interactions between different groups, societies, nations or civilizations, without ever trying to identify what are the factors determining their internal structures, thus, ignoring the nature of the forces operating within them. Using Toynbeean terminology, we should have to say all we have done is an "external" analysis. The second, broader analysis we have skipped, in fact, contains the first. It has also to do with the structure of our societies, but accounting for the fact that our species is roughly equally divided into two different sexes.

# 12

# THE LIMITS OF THE ECONOMIC SYSTEM

## Fixed Social Structure

Ever since Malthus pointed out our propensity for demographic growth as the sole cause for all poverty and social evils, no other theory has thrown a definitive light on this important subject.

In the surplus economy of the United States, according to their Census Bureau, 34.5 million people lived behind the poverty line in 1988,[22] this, according to the different poverty thresholds defined by the Bureau for that year, which for an unrelated individual, was an income below $8,316 dollars a year.

Every politician campaigning for the presidency of his or her country, will make such promises as ending (or at least, decidedly fighting) poverty, criminality and vice, and will offer likewise, a better distribution of the income, more and better jobs, education, housing and health services, etc. And, for as long as civilization exists, the peoples of every nation will listen eagerly to such offers, forgetting that these issues have been a matter of promises for centuries, without any substantial progress ever actually occurring.

This state of things cannot be the product of chance. In all likelihood, such phenomena are the product of the social structure itself.

## Normal Distribution of Aptitudes—Unequal Distribution of Income

A distribution graphic of different human characteristics such as the height, weight, visual and hearing acuteness, and intellectual quotient, will show a Gaussian curve, also known as the normal probability curve, which has a bell shape with symmetrical sides. If we instead measure personal wealth, the curve will lose its symmetry and show an abnormally large quantity of individuals possessing very little wealth, and abnormally large personal wealth concentrated in a tiny sector of the population. And then the part of the curve showing the personal wealth closer to the average will appear, by comparison to the rich sector, displaced towards the poor end.

Economists use two measures of economic well being, wealth, and income. Both follow a fairly similar distribution. During 1977, in the United States[23], the richest 1 percent of the population owned 39.10 percent of the property. The next richest 4 percent, 22.30 percent (so that the richest 5 percent would own 61.40 percent of the property); the next richest 5 percent, 11.40 percent (so that the richest 10 percent would own 72.80 percent); the next richest 10 percent, 11.50 percent (so that the top 20 percent would accumulate 84.30 percent of the property); as for the next 40 percent, it owned only 15.20 percent, and the lowest 40 percent, could barely proclaim itself the owner of the 0.5 percent of all property within the United States. As for income, its distribution showed to be somewhat more benign. Income within the United States for the year 1977 had the following distribution by quintiles (each quintile representing 20 percent of the population): top quintile, 47.2 percent of the income; 4th quintile, 23 percent (the two top quintiles accumulating 70.20 percent of the income); 3rd quintile, 15.7 percent, 2nd quintile, 9.9 percent, and the bottom quintile, 4.2 percent.

What do these facts mean?

For any epoch and civilized group, we will find true the proposition that society has rewarded each of its individuals differently. In ancient times, we can suppose that authoritarian rule and rigid social customs produced huge inequalities from the disproportionate power enjoyed by kings, princes, noblemen, and the top ranks of the military and religious. Money and wealth would have then, followed social status. Modern economists often point (proudly) how this situation has been reversed. Now, they say, it is social status that follows money, meaning that the individuals getting the biggest rewards are those making the largest contributions to their economies. Following this line of reasoning, we could also add that, in ancient times, large sectors of the population were forced to work as slaves, serfs, servants, soldiers and all kinds of unskilled laborers, or freemen barely paid for their work as craftsmen or skilled laborers. Today no one is forced to work in any position, and the services of the individuals are rewarded to them by a system that competes for labor force.

It is under this state of things—presented to us as abysmally different from that of ancient eras—from which the majority of the population within developed countries keeps wondering about the cause of the inequities still plaguing their societies. This issue is especially disconcerting for a country that, like the United States, because of having only four centuries of significant demographic history, could be envisioned as "new," and nevertheless, reproduced the same unequal social structure.

There are, without doubt, technical proposals to end poverty and unemployment and minimize vice and crime, through the redistribution of income via taxation. But the "tax the rich" proposal (endorsed by Dr.

Wolff, among others), has, however, known limitations. Taxing the wealthiest sector of the population beyond a certain point, discourages them to invest, leading to a contraction of production, ending in a net loss of the fiscal revenue intended to fight poverty and unemployment.

When, by decree of a central authority, income was distributed evenly in Soviet Russia, poverty, unemployment, vice and criminality, were in effect checked. (Their income distribution showed to be similar to that of less-populated developed countries.) The disappearance of such a regime indicates us, however, that the Soviet society was paying too steep a price for these advantages, namely, the loss of all its liberties. When liberties were reinstated, poverty, unemployment, vice and criminality, returned too.

Why is it that all civilized societies, regardless of eras, show roughly the same degrees of social inequality? (Though the larger the population, the greater the size of the inequalities.) The Darwinian principle that there are not two individuals equally fitted, might be the answer to this enigma.

## Individual Differences as the Cause of Social Stratification

By definition, even a normal distribution of aptitudes would allow some occurrences both in the low and the high sectors. In animal societies, such individual differences induce a social stratification, though if measured statistically, they would never come close to the disproportions we can observe for civilized societies. Among human societies, the primitive ones either have a much more benign degree of social stratification or none at all, as in the case of all hunter-gatherer groups. Within pre-civilized societies, when some form of authority exists, it is rarely used to force anyone into anything, but rather directed towards creating consensus, solving disputes, and in sum, containing disruptive forces.

The previous considerations mean, however, that the more accentuated social stratification observable in civilized societies must share the same biological origin.

Supposing every human group having the same probability of producing abnormally gifted individuals, the chances to produce a bigger number of such occurrences increase proportionally with the size of the population. While a bigger number of occurrences of abnormally ungifted individuals would have no impact on the distribution of such economic variables as wealth and income, an absolute bigger occurrence of abnormally gifted individuals would indeed cause this distribution to lose its normalcy.

Let us think of science.

What percentage of the population belonging to all eras of the humankind has produced our scientific knowledge? It is very likely that if produced, a distribution graphic of scientific aptitude would be even more asymmetric than that of the wealth, showing for example, that less than 1 percent of the population of all eras has provided us with more than 50 percent of our scientific knowledge.

In fact, without individuals such as Heron of Alexandria, Archimedes, Galileo, Copernicus, Darwin, Newton, Lavoisier, Einstein, Planck, Freud and Mendeleyev, to name a few, we would lack scientific knowledge. It is not an uncommon occurrence in science that two different individuals come up with the same theories (sometimes at the same time). So, it could be argued that if the names listed above were erased from history, other names (like those of Alfred Russell Wallace or Gottfried Wilhelm Leibniz) would have replaced them. But, since we can consider that the alternative names would belong to individuals equally gifted as the ones that were actually recorded by history, the point here is that no number of average individuals could have reproduced their feats.

If, by decree of a central authority, all science, business, music, literature, sports, etc., were done by average-gifted individuals, we can easily imagine the low degree of development that such a system would produce. In very much the same way, if we deleted all the names in classical music having the same importance as those of Mozart, Beethoven and Wagner, what would be left?

These observations vindicate the admiration of Toynbee (and his countryman philosopher Bertrand Russell) for the individuals that according to Toynbee's views, constitute the "creative minorities" within every civilized society.

So, it is no wonder that a small group of especially gifted individuals will always, as according to popular perception, "get the lion's share," when placed in a community presenting comparatively little competition for them. Though, using economic theory, we should rather state that such gifted individuals actually produce their share. While doing so, they generate also wealth and income for many others (no Mozarts would mean no classical opera, leading to no opera houses, no big orchestras, no big interpreters, no elaborated stages and fancy costumes, and last but not least, no fun).

By extending figuratively this economic view to other abnormally gifted individuals, we could also point that, if the "work" of individuals such as Jack the Ripper could be measured in economic terms, they would deserve an absolute negative retribution. This way of thinking would add a negative sector to the curve of distribution of income, making it lose even more of its normalcy.

## Creative Minorities

Let us see in more detail the phenomenon of the "creative minorities," or dominant ones, if we prefer so. How is it that these minorities are created? Starting from zero, we would have to suppose that the individuals possessing more ingenuity, boldness, shrewdness, persuasiveness, persistence, and even ruthlessness or voraciousness, would have a bigger chance to be part of these minorities than other individuals presenting the same features in a lesser degree. Once established, we could suppose that these minorities would preserve themselves by inheritance, as they passed on to their offspring their genetic traits, social status, or both (thus supporting the popular perception about the people on the top being always the same).

Should we compare the names of ruling families, outstanding entrepreneurs, remarkable scientists or musicians, presidents, etc., in different generations, we would know otherwise. Though the people on the top always share the same features, their names keep changing.

The course of a few generations is enough to dethrone royal lineages and impoverish the descendants of tycoons. Science and art are even tougher fields. We rarely see a couple of say, father and son, being regarded as equally distinguished physicists, chemists or biologists, or musicians, writers or painters. We do not owe to "Newton the 1st," one of the developments of calculus, to "Newton the 2nd," the first principles of optics, to "Newton the 3rd," the classic laws of movement, and to "Newton the 4th," the first theory of gravity.

In sum, such cases as Johann Strauss the Elder and Johann Strauss the Younger, both accomplished musicians, are rather the exception than the rule, thus, the names of today's most famous millionaires, scientists, politicians, scientists, artists, and sportsmen, are not the same than those of past generations.

How is it then that these "creative minorities" preserve themselves (in characteristics) trough the course of the generations?

The short answer is that they renew their ranks from the most apt individuals in their respective fields, regardless of their social status.

This ability of the "high class" to preserve itself is in fact, a property all of the classes within a society have, thus producing through the ages, scarcely modified versions of the same social structure.

The vertical mobility implied on the preservation of the "creative minorities" involves a small proportion of the population, and in fact, all vertical mobility seems to apply to the lesser part of the population within each social status.

Why is this?

## Social Selection Mechanisms

We can view the process by means of which all the social classes retain their basic features, generation after generation, through a mechanism we can refer to as "social selection."

As a teenager, I once noticed the girls using public transportation were less gifted than those riding in luxury cars. I asked myself: *Why do beauty and money mix?* The answer is that, within a social environment, any qualities act as a magnet for others. A successful man is more likely to choose for a wife, a beautiful rather than an ugly woman, thus their offspring probably combining their qualities. An average man would also prefer to marry a young, intelligent, beautiful and charismatic lady, but because of his condition, he would probably end married to a woman as little gifted as himself, thus inheriting to their offspring their same disadvantages.

This mechanism is more extended than we could imagine at first sight. A personnel recruiter will discard without remorse the dozen applications piled over his or her desk, except for the one belonging to the lucky person chosen to fill the only vacant position. The same can be expected from a woman wanted in marriage, about rejecting all but one of her suitors. An American university claiming to produce the best graduates in the country was once cleverly criticized, since its admittance procedures guaranteed that only the best candidates nationwide could get in their classrooms.

It is no wonder, then, that millions of human beings routinely losing their opportunities to other individuals being younger, smarter, or more beautiful, creative, hard-working, charismatic, etc., will end and stay for good, at the bottom of the social ladder. Once there, many of these individuals, conscious or not of the rejection of the rest of the society, will feel encouraged to take some form of revenge.

It is only obvious that any sum of efforts to change this state of things, including subsides to public services or programs, or legislation granting equal access to jobs, education or information, etc., will never be enough. A society that privileges excellence will necessarily relegate its less gifted individuals to its bottom ranks. No one wants dumb doctors, drunken airline pilots, cowardly military men, or accountants that will make us pay more taxes than we have to.

So, it is only fair to say that all social stratification has a biologic origin. By this view, the position of a single individual within a less-populated society, is now represented within societies thousands or millions of times more populated, by entire social classes, which preserve their characteristics indefinitely through the action of social mechanisms occurring spontaneously.

## Limits of Redistribution Mechanisms

Extrapolating implications within this line of argumentation, it is not unlikely to suppose that ancient societies checked poverty, vice and criminality, using not only brute force, but also more benign methods. The construction of the pyramids of Egypt, regarded as an example of how the authoritarian Pharaohs commanded entire armies of slave laborers to do the harshest kind of work, could be reinterpreted as an act of massive hiring. Certainly, within a surplus economy possessing a high productivity agricultural sector that could sustain a much larger population, such great works might have made the difference between life and death, employment and unemployment, misery and relative wellness, etc., for thousands of individuals. The same can be said of the Roman strategy of providing "bread and circus" to the urban masses of dispossessed peasants, displaced from their rural environment by the establishment of large private estates—the latifundia—run with slaves by rich owners.

The Toynbeean process by means of which the "creative minorities" are turned into mere "dominant minorities" seems to have more to do with the relative abundance of employment, rather than with leaders losing their creativity. We can suppose the golden ages of civilizations coinciding with the realization of large projects meaning occupation for all of its population, the most able men being employed as architects, designers, directors, managers, foremen, etc., with little police work needed. Conversely, when a society is mostly built up, so that no major enterprises are carried out, rulers have to rely mostly in authoritarianism to keep the idle and dispossessed masses under tight control.

All of the previous considerations show us that the chronic (if not only) economic problem throughout history has been that of distribution, and so it remains in contemporary times. The Great Depression that affected the United States between the years of 1929 and 1939, left 13 million people, most of them able men and women, without anything to do. Yet, the United States of that time had unrivaled means of production. As the First World War ended and Europe resumed agricultural production, thousands of farmers lost their huge overseas market. Facing lower prices at home, they turned to overproduce (at a time when overproduction was the very problem) to compensate for any loses. This started a cycle of deflation that first indebted the farmers and later broke them. Once bankrupt, besides being unable to pay for their bank debts, the agricultural sector, which was an important part of the economy, stopped its consumption of a good deal of goods and services, causing the closure of many commercial and industrial business. As no money was being spent either by the government (who was afraid to do so), or by private entrepreneurs (because of the gloomy perspectives), part of the system just halted. Even before English economist John Maynard Keynes presented in 1936 his work *"The General Theory of Employment, Interest, and Money,"* outlining a solution for the Depression (by means of public spending), President Roosevelt's administration was already helping some of his countrymen by giving them a way to earn some money. In spite of some progresses, by 1939 the United States' economy had not been totally recovered. It was the outbreak of the Second World War that provided Roosevelt with the reason he lacked to totally unleash the power of public spending.

In these days all these economic mechanisms are well understood, and the ancient redistribution means have evolved into the fiscal and social security systems, as well as into programs designed to fund public education, health and housing, etc. The previous implies, however, that all economic systems have well-known limitations that cannot be tackled by any redistribution mechanisms.

What is the direction our economic systems will evolve into? Surely, we will try to improve them, either consciously or unconsciously, making them more effective. But in all likelihood the "effectiveness" we are talking about, will have a different meaning. It will not just be producing more, in less time, with higher quality, at lower prices, etc., which is something we might think we are already good at. A really effective economic system would have to solve the distribution flaws we have mentioned above. And the best—if not the only—way to cope definitely with any misdistribution problems is to avoid their generation.

# 13

# THE LIMITS OF CIVILIZATION

## Civilized Behaviors

When comparing the civilized behavior with that of the "savage" or primitive peoples, we find the civilized one being really much harsher. In today's civilized societies we see many social layers, the difference in privileges between those at the top and those at the bottom, being abysmal. Individual and group differences are deliberately emphasized through a wide variety of customs that are best reflected in the ways we dress, address to others, or make use of specific or restricted areas. Competence between individuals is much more aggressive, and the number of homicides is an eloquent indicator of this fact.

As children, we are encouraged to become leaders, goal oriented and successful individuals. In many cases, comparative advantages on the side of the more "visionary" or "witty" individuals and/or groups will be translated into the conscious or unconscious exploitation of the disadvantages of other individuals or groups.

Relationships between the individual and society turn to be very complex. The formally regulated behaviors, those specifically covered by legislation, fill entire libraries. But legislation represents only the part of the social codes that, because of their importance, cannot be trusted to individual or collective memory. Thus the whole extent of the social codes recognized by a civilized society is much larger than its written fraction. In effect, this abundance of social codes reveals the great number of possibilities in which individuals can behave wrongly.

Personal failures are common. Civilized societies have long disposed of such failures through institutions such as orphanages, foster homes, mental hospitals, asylums, reformatories, jails, and even convents and nunneries have been used for such purposes. When, according to the customs or legislations in use, the individual failures deserve so, they meet their final fate in the hands of executioners.

Only large concentrations of human beings make possible the individual's isolation in the middle of crowded places or their own neighborhoods. Take orphaned children, parents who have lost children to death or other worldly circumstances, homeless families, abandoned wives, single mothers, lonely widows and widowers, elders with no one to see after them, illiterates, alcoholics, drug addicts and perverts. They are all part of the everyday dramas filling newspaper pages, the time on newscasts, or the story lines captured in movies.

Within complex societies, the individual does not have to do anything special to attract the aggression or criticism of others. In fact, no one, male or female, poor or rich, child, adult or elder, is exempt from disadvantageous conditions. Individuals often find themselves envying someone else's privileges, or feeling disillusioned by comparing their present condition with that of themselves, in past of future times. Children wanting to be grown-ups, grown-ups whishing they could be children once again, graduates yearning for their lost freedom as students, university students dreaming to already be graduates, bachelors complaining about their loneliness, married man envying the liberties of bachelors, etc., are all reasons for personal dissatisfaction.

Though none of this is new, as the ancient Greeks complained too for the loss of simplicity the earlier ways of life had, we should ask ourselves if the complexity of life in our societies has any foreseeable limit. Many see this increased complexity in such trivial facts as the number of ice-cream flavors, the pages of a newspaper, or the available local TV channels, jumping within a few years from say, 40, to 80.

## Individual Failures Coming from the Average Sector

Others find a more serious source for concern in the fact that the individual failures are now coming from within the less-likely sector of the population, that of the "normal" or average people.

A hard-working man can go berserk, fetch a weapon and start shooting. Getting laid-off, left behind by his wife, losing his savings, finding an unexpected deduction on his paycheck, discovering that his TV set is missing upon arriving home, or learning that his dog has been mistreated by a neighbor are each scenarios that can push a man over sanity's edge. He will shoot most likely against those people he regards as being responsible, co-responsible, or co-participant of his loses, and that may include his wife, children, close relatives, neighbors, boss, co-workers, or the people gathered at a wedding, family or school reunion. Thus, an increasing number of individuals find themselves living at the very limit of their tolerance, and this unfortunately, does not exclude children, adolescents or elderly people.

Why is stress and depression showing a steady increase within our societies?

In a civilized environment, happiness is frequently identified with the achievement of difficult goals, such as the accumulation of wealth, the gain of personal recognition or status, and sometimes, the creation of a happy family.

But a number of these goals are in practice, unreachable, contradictory, or deceiving.

By definition, meritorious goals (which are pursued by many) will be achieved only by a limited number of individuals. The consolation for the majority that will never get close to reach one of the pursued goals is often not socially accepted, as lowering one's expectations can be identified with mediocrity.

Expectations are contradictory too, when a man works hard for his family, and because of it, he rarely gets to spend time with them, thus, becoming a stranger to the very people he intends to make happy.

Expectations may also behave as mirages. When an individual finally reaches one of his or her purposed goals, he or she might find, however, that the achieved goal is either not good enough, or that it was the wrong kind of goal.

Thus, technology, which was supposed in other times to help us all in achieving personal wellness, is unable to make any difference. For as long as society sets goals for each one of us, and then, by individual evaluation, determines successes and failures, the rate of success will remain roughly the same, or, should the goals be getting harder to obtain, the proportion of failures will actually increase. This phenomenon—low rates of personal satisfaction—is especially disconcerting as it affects more, within developed counties, those that are already experiencing depopulation, as the rates of suicide among some developed European nations show.

## Uncivilized Behaviors

On the other hand, thanks to the work of modern anthropologists, we have a detailed picture of life within contemporary hunter-gatherer societies.

Contrary to popular belief, the individuals belonging to these societies lead easy and comfortable lives, and enjoy life-spans comparable to ours Anyone new to the subject, will be amazed by Leakey's or Pfeiffers's accounts of well hunter-gatherer peoples actually do, lacking nothing they consider useful.

Among these groups, individual differences are deliberately minimized. (On one occasion, I got to see a documental on Amazonian tribesmen. A Western doctor came to see a group of male hunters, all of them looking about the same age, wearing the same garments, tattoos and ornaments, with their hair-dos resembling a helmet. As the doctor tried to apply an injection to the one of them who was sick, all of his healthy peers asked for the same treatment.)

Although disputes exist and murders occasionally happen, we can easily regard such people as the Kalahari's !Kung (formerly called Bushmen), belonging to the San peoples, as leading one of the most pacific and fulfilling ways of life known. Since they fear violence, their most common strategy to avoid conflict is by moving away, which is something they are used to do, danger or not.

As everyone is encouraged to resent being told what to do (a usual reproach to a peer is to call him bossy), there are no bosses. No one gets orders or gives them, and even benign leaderships are ephemeral. Children rarely get spanked or punished, and individual competition is mild when compared to civilized standards.

Individual arrogance is discouraged by strict customs. As some hunters are better than others, a very successful hunter, especially if young, could feel the entire band depends on him. Coming to the campsite announcing a big kill would is, thus, considered rough behavior. The correct etiquette of a successful hunter is to sit at his fire and say nothing until someone approaches him. When questioned, he must complain about his own incompetence. The more he downplays his performance, the bigger the prey was. Upon returning to the campsite with the prey, other hunters will say he needed no help at all to go retrieve such a small animal, and the hunter must agree vehemently (the now very rare eland, the largest kind of antelope, can exceed 600kg).

The hunter whose arrow hit the prey distributes the catch among his group. However, that individual is not always the same person that actually shot the arrow. The distribution is done according to strict customs that ensure every one gets a share, following lines of kinship, alliances and obligations. The food coming from the women's gathering activities is brought back at the campsite, and shared too.

An invisible net, of relationships of kinship, friendship and obligations, keeps the organization between all bands neatly close. Socialization is intense. Though campsites are temporary, sometimes lasting less than a month, they are usually erected one close to another. During the dry season, when all temporary water holes dry, bands concentrate at the several permanent water holes, in numbers exceeding 100 individuals.

Large-scale trance-dances, initiations, cures, intense story-telling episodes, gift exchanges, and marriage brokering take place. The bands leaving the yearly concentration not necessarily have the same composition. The annual event provides them with the opportunity to choose with whom to live for the better part of the year, thus allowing any tensions to dissolve. Most individual disputes are solved before they have any chance to get serious. People's conversations are public property, thus, any problem arising is solved quickly through communal jokes.

Women provide most of the food for most of time, mainly from vegetable sources, which is why meat, amounting to about a third of the hunter-gatherer's diet, is so appreciated. While males typically hunt in couples, perhaps with a single apprentice, and most of the time, with poor results, gathering is a much more reliable source of food, which is carried out by all of the women and their children, leaving no one behind at the campsite. Any woman, not necessarily the mother of an infant, can prevent a quarrel by simply separating the would-be antagonists, which is something that is done casually, without interrupting any conversations.

No child ever gets the satisfaction to make another one cry. As sharing is essential to their way of life, infants are conditioned by such practices as being given string beads that they keep for a few months, and when provided with new ones, they are encouraged to pass the old ones to a relative.

Much of the previous features are not exclusive of the !Kung, as all contemporary hunter-gatherers lead similar ways of life. Anthropologists often mention "magic numbers." Worldwide, hunter-gatherers are composed by bands of about 30 individuals, while their bigger tribal units—all of the bands speaking the same dialect and sharing the same customs—rarely exceed 500 people.

In general, 20th century anthropologists views differ from that of their 19th century predecessors, in about the same degree modern chemistry diverges from the phlogiston theory. Here are statements about hunter-gatherers that are not unusual now. *The hunter-gatherer society is the original affluent society, in which all wants are easily satisfied. The mind of the hunter is essentially the same as that of the scientist's, because the hypotheses inferred from animals tracks are constantly assessed for their merits and often have the chance to be checked against fresh evidence. The hunter-gatherer way of life provides more leisure time than any other form of human social organization yet evolved (as quantitative studies have revealed). The religious beliefs of some hunter-gatherer groups are among the most elaborate known. An average hunter-gatherer's knowledge is enormous, as it often regards even the tiniest features about his lands, plants and animals, as well as the names of hundreds of places he has known, either first-hand or through the descriptions of peers. Western biologists or pharmaceutical companies often turn to hunter-gatherers either to corroborate bizarre findings or develop new drugs.*

In short, should we try to consciously design an optimal form of social organization, it would be difficult to catch up with the hunter-gatherer's naturally evolved way of life, which is one that has remained stable for millions of years, even before we got to be human.

# 14

# MARX'S FORGOTTEN CONTRIBUTION

## Universal Social Forces

So far, we have identified the limitations of our economic systems, that is, specified the tasks they can and cannot perform, as well as pointed the many disadvantages that come with the civilized way of life. Now we must ask ourselves if there are any forces capable of reshaping such structures. Many would consider this question an idle one, though. Economic systems and civilizations have evolved all the time, so we should expect many more changes still to come.

But this is hardly the point.

A majority, if asked, would regard civilization to be the definitive form of social organization of the humankind, one that would last for as long as humanity does. We have reasons, however, to think that the same forces that have shaped our modern societies will continue to operate with the same strength—if not more, or rather, at a faster pace—as today. Their actions are capable of much more than just improving our present social structures and way of life. More likely, civilization will continue evolving to such a degree until it reshapes itself beyond any recognition.

What are these forces?

So far, we have been paying attention mostly to technology. Technology is certainly responsible for much of the reshaping of our ways of life. But if we only took technology into account, we would be missing about half of the picture.

Strangely enough, this also happened to Toynbee. By focusing his attention into the action of his "creative minorities" and ignoring the role of the masses, Toynbee missed the very mechanism that explains the transit from authoritarian systems into gradually more liberal ones. In very much the same way as technology occurs as response to needs, the existence of social inequities triggers equally powerful social responses.

As a high-school student, I had trouble in digesting the fact that king Louis XVI of France was dethroned and guillotined by his own people. How could a reigning king, one that had commanded the army and was always surrounded by a corps of heavily armed guards, end executed in front of the populace? The same disbelief pervaded me when I learned how Czar Nicolas II fell captive to the Bolsheviks, who executed him along with the whole of his family.

But the most impressive social transformation I actually had the chance to witness, was the fall of Soviet Russia. Very much in the fashion of Toynbeean processes, which always come from within the civilized society and constitute the better part of their "life," Soviet Russia collapsed on its own, with no ostensible external forces determining this final outcome.

What caused the demise of the Soviet system?

Incredibly, the man who in turn, centered his analysis on the nature of the social processes resulting from the action of the majorities and introduced us to the concept of "class struggle," Karl Marx, misinterpreted its own principle.

The most likely explanation for this, is that Marx—though him in a much greater degree—the same as Malthus, instead of being concerned mainly (or only) with the enunciation of precise, general principles, aimed to reform society itself. Without doubt, Marx was a great thinker that devised an extensive theoretical frame to explain the action of majorities throughout history, as well as the workings of economics.

But Marx also devoted much of his time and energy to actively pursue the instauration of a "dictatorship of the proletariat," which is something only contradictory. Spontaneous processes occurring either in nature or in human societies, need no promoters, as (the very meaning of "spontaneous" implies) they happen on their own. So, just like Malthus, Marx failed miserably in his predictions, this time, about a dictatorship of the proletariat ruling forever.

## Struggle of Classes

For our purposes, we will accept the concept of "struggle of classes" as an historical constant, thus affecting all civilized societies, regardless of ages. Under our conception, all social forces promoting social change can be envisioned as class struggles. The classes are segments of the population within a society experiencing a pressure that moves them into action against other classes responsible or suspicious of being the source of the pressure exerted over them.

A class struggle doesn't constitute a need for a class to actually demonstrate the existence of a pressure in objective or legal terms. The sole perception of any inequity will create this pressure, making it real. The goal of every class struggle is to get rid of what ignited it, things like inequities, imposed restrictions, taxation, exploitation, unfairness, prosecution, etc. By this definition, both the classes and their struggles cease to exist with the achievement of the pursued goals.

For instance, a "slave class" will organize rebellions or assume a position of passive resistance, only while the pressure exerted upon them is still active. If, however, slavery is abolished for good, so slaves should no longer exist, they dissolve as a "class" and so does their struggle. On the other hand, class struggles are endless because there are no known civilized societies without inequities. So, for the better part, class struggles do not disappear, but just evolve.

If, on the case of former slaves, some form of discrimination subsists against them, they will continue with their struggle, this time, seeking the end of any discrimination because of their previous status.

Class struggles show the same cumulative patterns of technology and standard of living. Thus, they always reduce the size of the original inequities, assuring their conquests in a way that makes the return of the original inequities from impossible to very unlikely.

Since their advancement is always in one direction, the outcome of these processes is predictable. Spartacus' quest, the third revolt of its kind within the Roman Empire, which sought to liberate all its slaves and cost Rome dearly, though failed, made the Roman society aware of the need to lessen the slave's burdens or risk further uprisings. Long after slavery vanished in Europe, it reappeared in North America. As we know, slavery in North America was also the cause of a big war. Interestingly enough, this time the slaves' cause triumphed by the evolution of the classes in struggle.

Instead of the slaves mounting large-scale military operations against their oppressors, the war was fought between abolitionists inspired by religious and cultural values, and slavery advocates who relied heavily on the slaves' manpower.

This shows us that though the final outcome is always the same, the means might evolve. If violence does not work for a cause, a Christ, Gandhi, Martin Luther King or Lech Walesa, will introduce us into offering the other cheek, civil disobedience, civil rights, or solidarity. In fact, Marx's struggle of classes, can explain the very downfall of the communist society he helped to create.

As the majority of the people under the communist regime lost all of their political and economic freedoms, and in spite of the social progresses (acknowledged by a large part of the Soviet population), they nevertheless, fought silently against the privileges of its "political class," eventually leading to its downfall.

Thus, far from leading to dictatorships, class struggles always succeed in destroying any kind of oppression or control exerted by a (privileged) sector of the population over others. The reason why some of these social changes surprise us is because they sometimes seem to happen suddenly. Actually, it may take decades, centuries—or even millennia, as we go back in history—for class struggles to produce any radical changes.

This is true regardless of the changes showing their effects overnight, so that we would be comparing today's situation against yesterday's. And it is true when looking at less dramatic changes accumulating over a extended period of time, so that we would compare, as an example, human or workers' rights in the 20th century, against those of earlier centuries.

The effect of technology on the outcome of class struggles is either neutral, or acts as a catalyst that can only slow or accelerate them.

## Self-correcting Nature of Class Struggles

Class struggles can too over-achieve their goals, thus making the "social pendulum" shift to the opposite side.

Let us think of a religion. Should a religion practiced by a minority be the cause of their prosecution, it could happen that the faith of the few would just be reinforced, thus, over the centuries, turning into a majority that would establish a new official religion.

But, should the new religious majority or their leaders assume the same role of its former prosecutors, then the struggle of dissatisfied minorities would eventually undermine the authoritarian rule. This could lead, for example, to the splitting of the new faith into a different and, therefore, opposed branch of the original religion.

Other example we can use, is that of syndicates. In fighting an initial inequity, labor unions can, on the long run, accumulate a great deal of power and use it to impose unfair conditions to their employers and gain political influence. In such an instance, all of the other "classes" within the same society affected by such negative effects as increased prices and unfair elections will push until the deviation is corrected.

So, our definition of a "social class" rather than applying exclusively to fixed segments of the population (for example, the high, the middle, and the low class), extends to cover any number of individuals actively (or by means of passive resistance) challenging whatever privileges other "classes" enjoy.

Democracy is only the most visible and universal effect produced by social struggles, as in all cases, concerns the overwhelming majority of the population.

Other "classes," however, may be composed by comparatively lesser segments of the population, for instance, homosexuals of either sex and any social status, fighting for the same cause, namely, that of the discrimination against their way of life by the heterosexual majority.

By this definition, a single individual may belong to as many "classes" as causes he or she defends. The common struggle of consumers, pensioners, ecologists (or rather, environmentalists), prison inmates, illegal immigrants, prostitutes, gun owners, non-smokers, etc., to defend what they see as their rights, unites them across such different social conditions as sex, age, race, status, nationality, etc.

Class struggles, as defined, can also gain the support of the most unexpected individuals as they may come from sectors of the population traditionally opposed in views. In all likelihood, it will be the action of the families of the victims, regardless of their political leanings, that will legalize the consumption of drugs (narcotics), thus taking the control of this issue away from the police, to health institutions.

The added effects of all of these social struggles, is already driving developed countries to what we could envision as an "omni-directional democracy," as not only political rights, but all kinds of rights, including those of minorities, are gradually acknowledged and respected.

Aside from what can be seen as these many "minor" struggles (as they affect less numerous sectors of the society), there is still another universal social struggle, thus, affecting the whole of the society. Precisely because of its universality, this cause bears a special importance to the human race.

# 15
# THE FEMALE OF THE SPECIES

Of the many examples of social struggles mentioned in the last chapter, perhaps the one that will shake (or is already doing it) our societies more than all of the others, is the quest of one half of the humanity to strip off of its privileges the other half. Women's centennial fight to conquest the roles traditionally reserved for males, such as high positions within politics, the government, the army, the church, the working force, science, the arts, etc., is well and alive, and its totally predictable triumph might lead the world into an unseen age of depopulation.

The "war of the sexes" to dethrone male dominance has already compromised, especially within developed countries, ancient institutions such as marriage, along with its product, family.

## Unequal Social Importance of the Sexes

Historically, the social importance of women has always been inferior to that of men. Obliged by custom to fidelity and obedience, devoted to serve their husbands, raise children and take care of the domestic work, women, in addition, have been disqualified to own property, becoming themselves the property of their husbands. Their duties have been extended to all of the males in her families; and have also been prevented from going to school, act on stages, vote or being voted, etc.

Women may not give their names to their own children, and have to change or modify their maiden names with the name of her husband, thus being commonly referred to as the wife of somebody.

Matriarchy, as well as polyandry, are rare exceptions. Women retain the higher hierarchies of their societies in rare cases such as the Tuareg peoples who live in northern Africa, and women who are married to several men (polyandry) are only seen in societies where most females are killed at birth. Even today, in some regions of southern India, many pregnancies are terminated as soon as the sex of the fetus is determined, thanks to sonograms, as being female.

Throughout most of history, the importance of individuals, with equivalent functions, has been very different according to their sex. We see this unequal importance in such male-female pairs as king and queen, doctor and nurse, boss and secretary, pilot and stewardess, priest and nun, and even actors are known to be better paid than actresses.

If we assume the intellectual ability of individuals to be randomly distributed, we should expect to see as many female geniuses as there have been male ones, and yet, cases as the one of Madam Curie, are rare. Without doubt, this has nothing to do with any lack of intellect on the side of women, but rather, with the fact that they have been reared to concern themselves with other (lesser) functions. Thus, this being a good example of the "nurture versus nature" debate, which in this case, obviously tilts on favor of nurture.

What are the reasons of this phenomenon? According to our method, we should first look for an answer in nature.

## Sexual Dominance in Nature

The most common rule applying to animal societies is the social superiority of either sex.

Male inferiority is evident in the cases in which males die immediately after fertilization, or are terminated by their females as soon as their sexual function is no longer needed. As we know, this happens among honey-bees and wasps, and female black widow spiders may devour their male after mating. A male wasp, which has successfully penetrated the female, gets its penis stuck into her body, separating only when its abdomen is ripped by the sudden twists of the female, thus dying immediately. Likewise, among bees, as drones are unable to feed themselves, all those surviving the mating season are driven away from the hive and left to starve. In the case of black widow spiders, a carnivorous species, only the female is venomous, thus even if surviving fecundation, it is hard to imagine how the smaller-sized male can defend and feed itself, as the venom is necessary to paralyze their prey. Within mammals, the hyena female produces more testosterone than the male, is stronger and bigger than it, and thus, dominates it socially.

For no evident reason, though, the majority of animal societies are male dominated. In total, Darwin conceived three principles of selection. Natural selection was his main working concept, but as we have already seen, he also devised the principle of human selection. Let us now take a glance at his principle of sexual selection (which also explains dimorphism, that is, the phenomenon regarding the males and females of the same species, looking strikingly different):

> "This form of selection depends, not on a struggle for existence in relation to other organic beings or to external conditions, but on a struggle between the individuals of one sex, generally the males, for the possession of the other sex. The result is not death to the unsuccessful competitor, but few or

no offspring...Generally, the most vigorous males, those which are best fitted for their places in nature, will leave most progeny. But in many cases victory depends not so much on general vigour, but on having special weapons, confined to the male sex. A hornless stag or spurless cock would have a poor chance of leaving numerous offspring...male alligators have been described as fighting, bellowing, and whirling round, like Indians in a war-dance, for the possession of the females; male salmons have been observed fighting all day long; male stag-beetles sometimes bear wounds from the huge mandibles of other males; the males of certain hymenopterous insects have been frequently seen...fighting for a particular female who sits by, an apparently unconcerned beholder of the struggle, and then retires with the conqueror. The war is, perhaps, severest between the males of polygamous animals, and these seem oftenest provided with special weapons. The males of carnivorous animals are already well armed; though to them and to others, special means of defence may be given through means of sexual selection, as the mane of the lion, and the hooked jaw to the male salmon; for the shield may be as important for victory as the sword or spear.

Among birds, the contest is often of a more peaceful character. All those who have attended to the subject, believe that there is the severest rivalry between the males of many species to attract, by singing, the females. The rock-thrush of Guiana, birds of paradise, and some others, congregate, and successive males display with the most elaborate care, and show off in the best manner, their gorgeous plumage; they likewise perform strange antics before the females, which, standing by as spectators, at last choose the most attractive partner... I can see no good reason to doubt that female birds, by selecting, during thousands of generations, the most melodious or beautiful males, according to their standard of beauty, might produce a marked effect.

Thus it is, as I believe, that when the males and females of any animal have the same general habits of life, but differ in structure, colour, or ornament, such differences have been mainly caused by sexual selection: that is, by individual males having had, in successive generations, some slight advantage over other males, in their weapons, means of defence, or charms; which they have transmitted to their male offspring alone."[24]

This mechanism suggests us first, that females will always get to be fecundated by the best males available (thus purging the species from the weak, unhealthy, ugly, etc.), and second, that all females have their reproduction assured, as the only ones at risk are the males.

As Darwin notes, competition is severest within polygamous animals. Apparently, the only mammals—apart from humans—who will fight to death for the possession of the other sex—in this particular case, entire harems—are the most massive seals such as the elephant seal, with only 9 percent of the males of this species achieving reproduction.

So, the probable reason behind sex dominance is not only that of guaranteeing reproduction, but also directed towards the successful rearing of the offspring until they are fit to survive on their own. Although there are species not relying into sex dominance, within mammalian societies this is the most common case, with male adults being destined to be socially superior to all of their female counterparts.

## Pair-formation in Monogamous Species

Among monogamous species, in addition to any other mechanisms for reproduction, the formation of couples is required. This special mechanism has not escaped the attention of ethologists, scientists specialized on animal behavior. In one of his many articles, Austrian ethologist Konrad Lorenz[25] deals with the process of pair-formation in ravens.

One of the first things he notes is that, when social statuses exist, as it is the case with ravens, all of the individuals can behave in both male or female ways. It will be the social status (and not the sex) of the individual, what determines its behavior; the individual behaving in the female manner being always the one with the lower rank. (Sex behavior may transcend sexes also in humans, as a male person will use a softer tone of voice and a politer attitude when addressing his boss or any superiors, and a female will display bossy or macho attitudes when reprimanding someone under her authority.)

Isolated ravens, notes Lorenz, always behave in the male manner, and hens, in the absence of cocks, will behave like the cock (such hens failing to lay down eggs).

If, however, two ravens are put in the same cage, the most vigorous (or in other bird species, the first one occupying the cage), will assume the male behavior.

Given such ambivalence, there is no way to find out the sex of any two individuals by simply placing them one next to another. An heterosexual pair with inverted behavior of ruffled grouse was formed by putting in a cage a strong female with a weak male, this couple producing no offspring because of the male's gonads proper function being inhibited.

In other of Lorenz' many accounts, he put two ravens in a cage, and the two immediately started to court each other, thus forming a pair. Later on, he let this couple out on the field, where an older tame male lived, and then, surprisingly, the raven acting as a male instantly turned itself into a female. This did not break immediately the love relationship of this female with (what turned to be) her original female partner, the estrangement between the two of them progressed gradually.

Now, how come among such ambivalent individuals, 50 percent of the pairs are not homosexual?

When dimorphism is a marked feature, any female is destined to be inferior in rank to all adult males, the male's plumage intimidating not only the females, but all of the other males as well.

According to Lorenz, heterosexual pairs are assured in the wild through the hormonally conditioned choice of a stronger or weaker partner. Lorenz states this scenario, providing that the bird at the apex of the rank is a male (should the highest-ranking female not find a stronger male within her colony, she would mate with another female).

So, it seems that—after other Lorenz' remarks contained in the same article—in the absence of well-marked dimorphism, it is only the greater vigor and activity, body size, weight, and aggressiveness, that serve to establish a "sexual who's who" among an entire colony.

Thus, sex roles and social status seem to be bonded together in most animal societies, with the female role being in most cases the subordinate one. This outcome probably has to do with the defensive function of the males, as dominant males may defend an entire troop even at the expense of their own lives, thus enhancing the chances of survival for all of the females and the young.

So it is the case among many mammalian societies, in which all males must be ready to defend their own social positions at any time, thus often creating disruptive forces. Meanwhile, the females often appear to be the stabilizing force, as they are far more sociable, maintaining closer relationships with a greater number of individuals of either sex (no female will ever abandon or be expelled from a group, as it is common with males).

## Mating in Solitary Species

Within much less gregarious species, such as bears, which establish territories and avoid each other, other mechanisms apply. When in heat, a female bear will release pheromones that can be smelled by males many kilometers away. Males attracted to the female will approach with care, as the hormonally excited female will be very aggressive. If a male is too young, old, weak or sick, he will probably decide not to approach further. If the male feels fit enough, he will proceed to a courtship resembling a wrestling contest, by means of which the female will assess the vigor and skills of the male. If the male turns out not to be a fair suitor, he will flee before the irritated female has more chance to hurt him. If instead the male passes the test, the female will accept intercourse, immediately after which the ephemeral pair will split. After the hibernation, when the female bear delivers her cubs, she will have to protect them, among other predators, against male bears who will not hesitate to eat such a tempting prey.

Now, what are the most likely effects should the traditional role of the sexes disappear within humans?

Using the animal examples as a reference, the effects surely would prove to be as disorienting, among societal species as ravens, as making all individuals, male or female, equally vigorous, active, aggressive, etc. As for solitary species, equally fitted individuals would make a female bear never to find a male being a fair match for her.

Using our own species as reference, we find that in past times, couples formed by socially unequal male-female partners, such as king and queen, doctor and nurse, boss and secretary, etc., besides being easily produced, usually left numerous offspring. On the other hand, in today's developed countries, we see many women simply choosing to pursue a career rather than to marry a man and depend economically from him.

In very much the same fashion, a woman with a steady income might prefer to get pregnant without marrying, taking care of her child on her own.

Also, even if pair formation is achieved—marriage involved or not—many women with good-paying jobs do not want to conceive, as pregnancy interferes with her work and disturbs her emotions as well as her social and sexual life.

So, within developed countries already experiencing depopulation, low marriage and low fertility rates are two phenomena happening at the same time.

In short, in past times, women were driven into matrimony simply because they were not expected to support themselves. Even if they had some access to employment, they were typically assigned to low-paying jobs. On top of that, women wanting to have sex often found marriage as the only socially accepted way to get it. Though marriage might still be an option to improve a woman's social status and standard of life, as the proportion of women taking occupations traditionally held by men is increasing steadily, less women are feeling the urge to marry for such a reason.

In fact, one might consider if ancient rich societies also underwent a phase of low fertility as all kinds of individual liberties were let to increase (or social customs lost their strength). Sodom and Gomorrah both appear to have been rich cities. Meanwhile, the ancient Greeks accepted homosexuality, the Kama Sutra depicts lavish and morally relaxed lifestyles that resemble very much those of Imperial Rome, and Malthus saw, within the newly formed United States, *"the manners of the people more pure... than in any of the modern states of Europe."*[26]

As it is the current trend affecting many well-paid jobs in science, research and development, and computerized analysis in industry and business, intellectual skills will chiefly determine who gets such jobs. Competing women, who typically are more dedicated as school grades often show, will actually have more chances of getting them than males.

Thus, in the not so distant future, under a panorama of increasing numbers of self-sufficient and independent women, marriage—which has never been easy—and family—that typically demands more maternal attention—will become rarer and rarer, so that birth rates well below the replacement level can surely be expected.

# 16

# THE END OF GROWTH

## Worldwide Decrease of Fertility Rates— Towards an All-Developed World

According to world population data (both historical and estimated) released by the United States Census Bureau for the one-hundred year period of 1950-2050, the rate of growth of the world population, after 1970, has been steadily diminishing. Starting with an annual population growth of 1.47 percent for the midyears of 1949-1950, the peak years of the period were 1961-1962 and 1962-1963, with global increases of 2.19 percent, each. The estimated growth for the year 2049-2050 shows the lowest global increase for all of the encompassed period, which is 0.43 percent[27].

This slowing is due to decreasing of fertility rates, especially within less-developed nations, which account for practically all of the world's population growth. These data are thus, consistent with the United Nations' estimate regarding the world's population stabilizing in about two more centuries.

Why are fertility rates declining in less-developed countries?

In past chapters we stated that the first symptom less-developed countries show when exposed to new technologies, is a steep increase in their population. Later on, as these countries assimilate more technology, their population tends to grow at a slower pace. In other words, as less-developed countries gradually transform themselves into developed ones, their demographic behavior changes accordingly, eventually stabilizing.

So, this is what is happening.

Decades ago, as all of the populations in the world, due to our enhanced technological means, entered in virtual contact because of the Second World War, the latest demographic explosion was produced.

Now, as all of the less-developed regions of the world are undergoing the same development process, their rate of population growth is showing a slowdown. This implies that in the not so distant future, all the nations of the world will be developed.

What an all-developed world will look like?

Let us go back briefly to our exploration of the phenomena occurring under ever-increasing and relatively isolated populations. Under such conditions we found, among other phenomena, that, first, sharp developmental differences appear spontaneously. Second, that previously isolated groups eventually make contact, thus leading to clashes among them. And third, that technological transference processes result in still greater increases of population, and such transference processes, when paired with differences in demographic behavior, make possible the constant rearranging of power statuses between different societies, thus allowing their relative rise or decadence.

Under constantly decreasing populations, we should expect all these phenomena to stop reproducing. So, the pressures responsible for most kinds of competition, the steep differences in living standards moving whole populations to overcome them, and rich nations that are supplied of everything from raw materials to workforce at cheap prices by other less-developed parties, are all possibilities that will vanish for good.

# Substitution of Competence by Cooperation

More important and immediate than the former, will be the displacement of competition by cooperation. In a still very populated world, inhabited by many different peoples marked by their cultural differences, war will remain as the greatest threat to all populations.

Though many see a faceless "global economy" as the force driving progress in all the corners of the world, what we see behind this "global economy" is the quest of the majority of the world population to level in living standards with their advanced counterparts.

Either way, no other phenomenon can damage a "global economy," or the living standards anywhere, as rapidly as war. Though we have no way of predicting any future wars, we can surely say that efforts to prevent them can only go in increase. Paradoxically, should such efforts fail, the bigger the damage, the more reinforced will these efforts reemerge. In these times, for instance, the possibility that the European states involved in the two world wars would clash again between them, is negligible.

Thus, it is no casual coincidence that a multinational state is emerging in the region of the world where close, frequent and unrestricted competition among equals, recently escalated to show some of its more devastating effects.

The European Union is the best example at hand on how competition will be gradually replaced by cooperation. If competition is the force that makes the parts collide between them, cooperation is a force very much like gravity. Within a geography where demographic stability has been achieved and all the neighbors share roughly the same degree of development, national boundaries are disappearing.

Sacred national principles, such as independence, sovereignty and self-determination, are giving way to greater common goals. Even commercial competition has found an adequate substitute by the economic specialization undergoing within the Union.

This new European covenant explicitly rejects any hegemonic intentions on the side of any of its member states. The Union' viability has not been compromised by the fact that some developmental differences still exist. The unified Germany has an economic weight no other of its allies can match.

But the Germans, who have been active promoters of the Union from the start, as well as the much more reluctant English, are nevertheless cooperating, because cooperation is much better than its older alternative, that of rivaling between them.

It could be argued that the real reason behind this new Union, is again, that of competing, as a unified Europe is much more economically competitive than its parts acting alone. Even if so, the striking difference, in this new alliance, is that predictably, the forces acting on its favor will endure.

In the past, European alliances were formed as easily as they were dissolved, according to the shifting interests of the parts. But in a region where all of the parts have long competed actively against each other to no avail, as none of them emerged as a definitive victor (in a sense, each one lost or was checked by all of the others), the common interests have eclipsed any surviving differences. The common interests have led to a wide politic, military, economic, technologic and financial cooperation.

In other words, under different conditions, the same parts are behaving differently.

The Union has proved to be a magnet for other European states. Since its humble origins of only six members in 1952, the European Coal and Steel Community evolved into an European Economic Community of twelve members, which was replaced later by an European Union that gained three more members, totaling fifteen at the moment. The Union has now thirteen more candidacies that include Turkey, a part-European, part-Asian country, with different culture and religion.

The same path of the European Union will surely be followed by many nations in other regions of the world where the same conditions—demographic stability and converging degrees of development—gradually make their appearance. However, there is more than just economic ease in development, as all contemporary developed countries share another equally important feature, namely, democracy, which acts as a homologating factor, making nations politically and socially compatible.

We see this trend towards regional cooperation in other parts of the world in the many treaties, such as the North American Free Trade Agreement (NAFTA), so far including Canada, the United States and Mexico. NAFTA, which started humbly as the early predecessor of the European Union, has sought limited economic partnerships between neighbors sharing the same continent.

## Multinational States

As such unions expand their original purposes, seeking higher degrees of integration (meaning less uncertainty for the parts involved), more multinational states will be created. With more than one multinational state, any affinity between two of such states will lead to the conformation of still wider federations covering regions of the world that could be as apart as America and Europe.

Where does this leave China and India in the international economic mix?

Any of these two countries would be on its own, more of an economic power than a possible pan-American-pan-European confederation.

Most likely, the notion of national power will change too. To start with, it is impossible not to think of a democracy being established in

China anytime soon. The events of Tiananmen Square back in 1989—the same year the Berlin Wall fell—would lead us to think the opposite, as the Chinese communist leaders showed to be as authoritarian as the most.

But even the Tiananmen Square protest had silent supporters within the Communist Party (some of them still in detainment). Furthermore, later developments revealed what the main concern of Chinese leaders was, namely, that of speeding up the process of China's economic modernization.

So, the reappearance of another event like the one in Tiananmen, might, just like the Berlin Wall, lead to the overnight collapse and substitution of China's communist regime with a democratic one, with little or no mayhem involved.

Should this feat not be accomplished in such a pacific fashion, it will proceed by more violent means. If the principle of struggle of classes has any validity, it will be the Chinese people themselves, with or without external help, who will get rid of any authoritarianism in their political system.

If no Western nation sees in India a potential foe, it is because unlike the Chinese, India did manage to establish a democratic system upon its independence. Partially because of this system not thwarting any liberties (India remains a mosaic of peoples having different religions and speaking thousands of languages), Indian progresses seem, by comparison to the Chinese, modest. It is not unlikely, however, that this situation might be leveled in the course of a few decades, as we can hardly imagine India being stalled indefinitely by whatever ethnical or religious differences.

With the two biggest nations in the world, that already share an equal interest to overcome their economic shortcomings, being governed by democratic systems, it is unlikely that they will be interested in quarreling with each other. Similarly, any hegemonic intentions on either side would be pointless.

Hegemony was unavoidable in a world with limited resources. Any hegemonic power was benefiting from its position, economically. As the resources used by future technologies will be practically inexhaustible, hegemony will serve to no purpose.

Now, is this the ultimate state of organization humanity will know, a global, unified democracy with global values and culture? We have reasons to think not.

# 17

# THE POST-CIVILIZED WORLD

## Civilization as an Evolutionary System

An implicit feature in our model of civilization is that of its inherent instability. A physicist would say this by stating that civilization is a "high energy" system. High energy systems can meet two fates, that of exploding, or losing gradually all of their energy, thus finally reaching, either way, their "most probable state," that of holding zero energy. For instance, our Sun's evolution started as a cloud of cold gas that contracted, heated, developed nuclear reactions, will run out of its nuclear fuels, and end as a black dwarf star, shining no more.

Physicians use too the term "evolution" when referring to the phases of a known illness or to a specific patient affected by it, and in the last case, the doctor can assess the prognosis as being either good or bad.

A biologist, when referring to evolutionary change, would point that species varying accumulate only the advantageous changes, thus, producing well-marked and divergent features.

The word "evolution" has been used also by anthropologists to differentiate the process of our biological evolution to that of our "cultural evolution," a phrase that makes reference to different stages of development common to different societies, or to the whole of humankind.

Except for the latter case, it seems clear that the term "evolution" refers to a well-defined pattern of changes affecting a system, taking it from an initial stage to a final one. The changes occur at certain rates, accumulating in an unidirectional sense (as they never go back), producing various intermediate stages identifiable with differences in the system's structure and behavior, with the changes in the final stage becoming imperceptible.

While making the analysis of our own history, we have become familiar with the idea of continued changes happening in a unidirectional sense and accumulating, as the ever-increasing levels of population, technology and standard of living show, resulting in different behaviors (our ways of life) that seem to be replaced at ever-faster rates.

Thus, what we lack, is an idea of what the final phase might look like. If our species is ultimately destined to perish, because of either being doomed to self-annihilation, a comet impacting the Earth, destroying all life, or an alien species invading from outer space, etc., such a fate does not concern us, this, not because of the improbability of such outcomes, but because of their complete unpredictability.

So, we will restrict our analysis to the one possibility of our species regaining an equilibrium in which changes occur either at a slow pace or in such a small degree that become negligible.

If we regard our "cultural evolution" as an extension of our biological evolution, barring major disasters, this is a very likely scenario. As a biologist would have no trouble in telling us, the process of biological evolution in our planet is very much done. This means terrestrial life is unlikely to reproduce the major changes that, starting with microscopic marine species, turned them into macroscopic ones that conquered land, evolving there into other distinct living forms, with some terrestrial species eventually developing the ability to fly, and others returning to marine environments.

Should a new glacial period was expected to come, a biologist would predict most species simply adapting to colder climates, and this would not mean evolution restarting anew. In stating this, the biologist would be acknowledging that the "most probable state" of the natural species inhabiting our planet has already been reached, meaning that most natural life on our planet will retain much of their present characteristics.

In regards to our history or "cultural evolution," most people would accept civilization being the "most probable state," or definitive form of social organization for the humankind. This would imply, however, according to our view of what an evolutionary process is, civilization having reached a stable stage, with all the major forces responsible for shaping it in the past, being now inactive. Yet, the rate of change of our way of living continues unabated with no sign of stabilization. What the conditions for stabilization are?

## Conditions for Stabilization

Should we identify man's ability to modify nature, that of its technological capacity, as the sole force responsible for the continued change in our population numbers, ways of life, and last but not least, of impacting our environment at a planetary level, then the condition for stabilization would be one in which further technological change, even if possible, is not likely to be produced.

But as we know, technology is not an independent force, as its action is inextricably linked to the levels that population show, as well as the behavior of populations towards their living standards. In other words, since we have showed that population growth—notwithstanding the fact that it is made possible only by technological means—promotes technological change on its own, in order to define a condition in which further technological development is not likely to be produced, we should seek for a condition of demographic stability.

Finally, as the goal of technology is to produce desired effects—all of them ultimately pursuing the enhancement of our standard of living—we should seek additionally for a condition in which all wants by all individuals within any populations, are effectively met.

Should we fall short, even in a small degree, of these conditions for stability—zero changes in population, technology and standard of living—proportional degrees of change should be expected.

Likewise, if instead of showing a tendency to level, these variables showed an unabated tendency to increase, we would be advancing towards a state of greater instability, thus, the system becoming more prone to liberate its excess "energy" in abrupt bursts (such as war), or even disintegrating for good.

Let us see now if a condition of demographic stabilization is likely to appear in the future.

As previously stated, demographic stabilization is achieved within individual societies through the action of unconscious mechanisms that divert both males and females from marriage and family. If we assume all future societies as developed, we should not expect only population stability, but instead, depopulation. Within this picture of development, one in which a status-seeking mechanism acts as the growth stabilizing force, its prolonged action eventually translating into depopulation, we have no way of clearly establishing if the rapidly progressing phenomena of empowered and independent women is already accounted for. If not, or if only partially accounted for, then we should expect even greater degrees of depopulation than those observed in contemporary developed nations. Because depopulation is neither an indicator of stability, we shall later ponder the issue of how long can we expect depopulation to go on.

For now, we have established that future generations are not likely to undergo further population growth. An immediate consequence of this is all future development of technology aimed to cover the needs of ever growing populations, stopping for good. Additionally, as, without exception, new necessities leading to new ways of life, have always appeared because of growing populations, under zero population growth or depopulation, the rate at which new needs are created should diminish until fading, ending in a stable way of life. To this, it could be very reasonably argued, however, that even under depopulation, all advanced contemporary countries are actively developing technology, thus, producing new commodities that reshape our way of life, as are the cases for instance, of microcomputers and cell phones.

Concurrent with this objection (if not the same) is the fact that the other force pushing technological development, the aim to reach ever-increased living standards, may never stop for good. So, any unfulfilled wants experienced by a group, demographically stable or not, would lead to the production of more technology. Within these unfulfilled wants, we should also account for those having a "psychological" or social nature.

Though so far technology has succeeded in raising the living standards of entire populations, it has not expedited their happiness in a similar way. This mean populations in developed societies are nevertheless experiencing different degrees of dissatisfaction (the most objective measure of economic well being, that of the per capita income, is known not to reflect over-all well being, which is in turn, a subjective appreciation). Thus, the highest effective living standard conceivable, would be one in which all individual wants, including those of a psychological or social nature, would be satisfied. This living standard would, therefore, imply the elimination of all inequalities flawing our economic systems, the disappearance of the unsolvable conflicts that have plagued civilized life in all epochs, and the consecution of women's goal to terminate with male dominance.

Should we fall short of a living standard so defined, so that populations would be granted to satisfy their every other needs, except for those affecting them in a psychological or social way, then, these unfulfilled needs alone would remain active. This would push them towards a condition in which all individuals would be equally rich, share the same social status, and lead easy lives. The motto adopted by the French revolutionaries concisely defined this goal in just three words: "Liberté, Egalité, Fraternité."

## Need for a Near-perfect Social Organization

Though this universal and millennial dream of humanity seems an impossible feat to accomplish, should we turn our attention to the past, we would find that a condition very much like this one was prevailing in human societies before civilization sprang. The—often characterized as "fossil"—way of life of the hunter-gatherers endurance' for millions of years points to a social organization without major flaws, otherwise, not only their small bands, but the entire human species would have vanished thousands or even millions of years ago.

A striking feature of hunter-gatherer societies is that, among all human societies, they seem to be the only ones that have no use for sexual dominance. As both sexes are allowed to be productive, no one has the chance to feel superior to the other, and yet, pair-formation is not inhibited. As for survival effectiveness, there is enough evidence to think we caused the extinction of many rival species during our long hunter-gatherer stage. The most remarkable case is that of a closely related species, that of the Homo Sapiens Neanderthalensis, commonly known as the Neanderthal man, which was sturdier than us, and probably equally gifted intellectually.

Regardless of its feasibility, a near-perfect form of social organization seems to be, however, a requisite for our preservation. If, instead of subsiding, social tensions became more acute so that individual failures would continue multiplying, any chances to assure safety within any human groups would vanish for good. This is an issue especially important for a future with enhanced technological means.

As we know, in these times, a small group of well-trained individuals can cause immense damage, and even a single individual equipped with a home computer can cripple dozens of commercial and governmental computer systems, all of which use the most advanced means of prevention against such kind of tampering.

In other words, especially in more recent times, destroying or disabling a system—such as a human body, or a city—has become increasingly easier. Though this has always been the case throughout history, many still believe that further sophistications will effectively prevent both mishaps and individuals with perverse intentions, from causing significant damage to any systems, persons, or societies. In fact, the exact opposite is true. As technology develops more and more complex systems, they show greater vulnerability to mishaps, tampering, or direct attacks.

Let us think, for instance, of atomic energy facilities. Their safeguards represent a major part of their design and operation costs, and accidents still happen. So, as the number of components that can fail multiply, complex systems' weaknesses are proportionally increased. Should we think of the human body as the most sophisticated system ever developed, we should point that its reliability is due not to clever, conscious engineering, but to millions of years of evolution driven by nature's blind trial-and-error process.

Thus, instead or far more complex forms of social organization, future generations will be forced to develop simpler, smaller, sparser, and more flexible social units. How possibly could all this be achieved?

The most likely answer lies where we started—in technology. The very factor, that promoted all change, will eventually reach a stage in which it will provide us with the conditions for stability. Let us see an example.

## Biological Homogenization

We have stated that social inequalities, within civilized environments, have a biological origin. Biological homogeneity among humans, as unlikely as it seems, is, however, an unavoidable (and unintended) effect of our never-ending quest for fighting disease.

Civilization changed some of our biological features, first for worse, and later for better, as compared to contemporary hunter-gatherers. Agriculture first weakened our health by substituting a much more varied diet with dependence on a few sources of food, promoting malnutrition. Animal domestication led to the surging of diseases only possible among dense human concentrations, where animals as distant in evolutionary terms as birds and mammals were kept together, allowing viruses and microorganisms to jump from one species to other, mutating, infecting humans, and spreading through courses of water as well as personal contact. As we know, these conditions have now been surmounted in the urban areas of developed nations.

In average, modern civilized humans are taller, healthier, and enjoy longer life spans than in the past. This is because of recent improvements on our diets and habits, as well as medical advancements both preventive and curative, such as vaccines and antibiotics. In a not so distant future, technology will provide us with much more advanced ways to prevent virtually all illnesses, including those caused by hereditary traits. As genetic procedures now make possible the prevention or treatment of previously incurable conditions, we see their use spreading.

Tissues from unborn babies can be taken from them, without compromising their viability—as in that stage they just grow more—which are later used to cure an older sibling. Likewise, some hereditary diseases can already be spotted in the earliest stages of development of a human embryo, allowing—through selection—the gestation of only healthy individuals, thus eliminating the undesired feature in future generations.

A map of all our genetic information will soon be completed under such endeavors as the Human Genome Project, and eventually, the unknown functions of many genes will be deciphered too. Thus, in the not too distant future, parents will be enabled to prevent their descendants from inheriting the traits that make them suffer from numerous health conditions such as mental illness, hypertension, arthritis, obesity, diabetes, etc. (Some geneticists have contended that all illnesses, including aging processes, are genetically determined.)

So far, we have been considering health issues, which provide the powerful reasons to experiment, and later make use, of advanced gene therapies. Throughout history, however, vanity has proven to be a powerful reason for individual dissatisfaction, this, to a degree of sometimes individuals bettering their looks at the expense of their health. In the past, the use of fine clothing, jewelry, wigs, cosmetics, perfumes, corsets, taller shoes, etc., improved somewhat an individual's appearance.

Under contemporary technologies, the same desires have evolved into surgeries, detachable or permanent implants, diets, exercise regimes and a host of other procedures. These technologies are much more effective in enhancing our looks by changing the color of our eyes and hair, whitening our teeth, diminishing or flattening bellies, getting rid of ugly noses or wrinkles, augmenting (or diminishing) females' breasts, increasing men's pectorals, fixing vision flaws previously corrected only with spectacles, etc.

But all these procedures do not help a short individual from remaining short, bald men from staying bald, women with wide hips still having to conceal them, or correct the body shapes of people with too short or too long trunks or limbs, etc.

As genetic techniques advance and proliferate, people will ponder besides health and looks, such issues as if low intelligence is not really the worst handicap of them all, so that instead of spending for decades on expensive schools, they should rather aim to improve their offspring's intellectual capacities. Though it is unlikely that "intelligence genes" may exist, a good overall constitution is probably linked to higher intelligence, as the general characteristics of the dominant individuals of both sexes within animal societies, often suggest.

So, future parents, wanting to have genetically enhanced descent, will be enabled to do so. Like all new technologies, procedures will be initially restricted to the wealthy, but as it is always the case, technology prices will eventually drop, enabling virtually anyone to have access to them.

Thus, the mere selection of desired genetic characteristics, discarding the unwanted, will cause an accumulation of the traits regarded as positive, making future generations to both diverge from their parent's characteristics, and converge between them, as there is not an infinite number of possibilities to genetically design near-perfect individuals. (Decades ahead of genetics becoming a field of its own, Darwin noted in his principle of "correlated variation," how certain traits are paired with other.)

So, individuals purged from any physical disadvantageous conditions will very likely resemble each other too, in psychological constitution. Genetic traits associated to race, resulting in different skin pigmentations, eye and hair color, facial features, etc. play a negligible role in producing better-fitted individuals, as intellectual skills, physical aptitudes, emotional balance, and many other psycho-biological features are independent from race. Thus, though the individuals of future generations may still look strikingly different, their overall psycho-biological features will be very similar because of their characteristics having being (unconsciously) homologated through spontaneous processes of selection.

## Gender Equality Regained

Technological advancement may also reach a stage enabling the restoration of the social equilibrium between the sexes. Whatever conditions were changed by civilization, making sexual dominance the prevailing form of organization among most human societies, if, in the future, both sexes are enabled to be equally productive (or neither one needs to be productive at all), no sex will have any reason to feel superior. Once this condition is reached, the struggle between the sexes should come to an effective end, and pair-formation, if yet needed, should be easily accomplished.

If for some reason, an imbalance should persist, then, science fiction has provided us with a number of extreme outcomes. To surmount the battle of the sexes, we are presented with scenarios in which all of the individuals of an alien species are either asexual or belonging to only one sex, mostly the feminine. In other cases, sexual functions have been lost for good, so that it does not matter to what sex an individual belongs to, since they have forgotten how to reproduce, or are unable or unwilling to do so. Many particularly anguishing questions—buried deep in our unconscious—surface and get answered in a number of ways, in science fiction scenarios.

When aliens are of a pacific nature, besides being very gregarious, status differences get smoothed over by them looking and behaving alike, and dissent among them is rare or inexistent. In other cases, individuals are linked through symbiotic relationships in which several of them are part of a greater being or force. Likewise, good-hearted aliens are all adults—thus sparing them from the trauma of coming of age. They have big eyes, with other facial features smoothed or minimized. They also have small mouths, noses and ears (as in the proportions of a child's face), and their behavior is naïve and affectionate, notwithstanding their enormous knowledge.

Aggressive extraterrestrials are often dimorphic. A single king, queen or emperor, with pronounced facial and body features, is strikingly bigger and much more aggressive than his or her submissive and numerous soldier-subjects.

In most cases, however, aliens seem not to wage wars among themselves, but rather, against other species, their intentions being either evil or noble. In a similar fashion, all the needs of the individuals of alien species seem to be completely fulfilled, as we rarely see them working, eating, sleeping, or going to the toilets, though they may need from time to time, to recharge their energies in different, cleaner ways.

Illness and death are deep concerns that get fixed too. Good aliens neither die nor get sick, or have regenerative powers capable of bringing them back to life after a temporary death, or, sometimes, their memory and personality are implanted on replacement bodies. Finally, somewhat cynical aliens often point out our backwardness as species, our environmentally disruptive behavior, and therefore, our uncertain chances to endure.

So, it is not aliens that are depicted in science-fiction scenarios, but us, most of the times, with all of our basic conflicts solved for good.

## The Last Stage of Technological Evolution

Now, what makes us think that further technological development will lead to the solution of virtually every disadvantage we are now subjected to?

Collective dreams never die.

They might have to wait for hundreds or thousands of years to become possible, but they are eventually achieved. Though flying was not precisely the most important of our collective wants, legends such as that of Daedalus and his son Icarus, who could both fly with wax wings, are a clear indication of how the ancient Greeks dreamed too of flying.

Thus, when the technological requirements for sustained flight were (barely) met, planes were developed. In the same way, we will take advantage of any circumstance enabling us to get rid of any unsolved issues troubling us. Because our present technologies, as compared to future ones, are as crude as we want to envision them, we still have many decades, or even centuries, of technological advancement. Before we reach a stage in which technology is ideally fitted to our needs and purposes, many other lesser flaws, as those affecting the best of our contemporary homes, will have to get solved.

Should we think of our need to be fed, we still remain, as Malthus once predicted, in *"the state of mixed pasture and tillage, in which with some variation in the proportions the most civilized nations must always remain."*[28]

We, thus, still deforest great extensions of land for agricultural purposes, and continue to sacrifice millions of animal lives, terrestrial and marine, for our consumption.

Is this the best we will ever be able to do?

Harvests are not exempt of carrying toxins such as residues of fertilizers and pesticides, as well as natural plagues. In order to get the most complex proteins contained in animal food, we can too ingest a number of various toxins, viruses and microorganisms causing different diseases, as well as saturated fats that will clog our arteries.

Similarly, most materials we use now for clothing can catch fire easily and will not protect us against but the most minor injuries. Transportation is still carried out by vehicles or vessels that are typically much heavier than the loads they are able to transport, and they are by no means exempt from causing or receiving significant damage from collisions. (The most advanced system of transportation imaginable would be, however, one in which no object having a mass would need to be transported.)

In the same fashion, most of the energy and water that we now produce is wasted along distribution systems. Again, the final users systems' take advantage of these resources with very low efficiency, as most energy is dissipated in the form of unwanted heat, and water is often spilled or used in large quantities for trivial purposes.

Thus, significant technological advancement is still possible because our present means are far from ideal.

Likewise, in order not to develop better forms of social organization, in which all individuals would belong in safe environments allowing everyone both to love and be loved, and yet, remain free from any undesired impositions, and in sum, lead harmonious lives fulfilled with companionship, art, science and wisdom, it would be necessary for us all to forget for good these ideals.

But, should our common ideal standards remain very much fixed through endless generations, it would be only incoherent to propose future societies evolving in any other directions, but the one leading to the achievement of the commonly pursued wants.

Now, here is one last consideration.

## Technology Versus Science

Should we stop producing technology—whatever the reason might be—would not we be defenseless against any threats coming to us from the outer space?; meteorites do impact our planet after all. In fact, one of the most widely accepted theories for the extinction of dinosaur life, is precisely that of one of such bodies colliding with the Earth where now is the Yucatan peninsula.

Do not we need constant challenges in order not to let our technological skills stagnate? Would not we more likely perish because of everyone forgetting how to deal with practical issues? Would not we experience decline, this time as a whole species?

Barring any disasters or irreducible imbalances, should we reach a stable way of living, with no further technological advancements being produced, we nevertheless, would retain our scientific capabilities.

Unlike technology, which is a response for needs as they arise, science is an answer to a permanent psychological need of the human race.

If the mental attitude of the greatest scientists of all eras is any good indication, they were all pursuing knowledge for the sake of knowledge itself. They all had fundamental questions about our universe, and felt the deep urge for no less straight and fundamental answers.

So they simply developed the answers, without mattering what their practical uses could be.

Should we now pose the question before a vast audience, about what the practical applications of Darwin's theory of evolution are (or for that matter, Newton's laws of motion), an overwhelming majority would remain silent.

Yet, the many seemingly aimless findings of our top scientists eventually proved to be of such relevance for technological purposes, that all technologies were forced to abandon their millennial trial-and-error approach, to follow the shortcuts allowed by the scientific method.

Because of this pervasiveness of the scientific method, technology is often confused with science, as popular expressions, such as "rocket scientist" and "computer science," unmistakably reveal.

Without any shade of doubt, much of the recent research aimed to technological purposes has fueled scientific knowledge in an unprecedented degree. But again, this is only due to the fact that modern technology does not stand a chance without the aid of the scientific method.

Should we need to characterize science and technology as having a different nature—as it is indeed the question right now—we should say that all science is universal, as its aim is to uncover the inner workings of nature, its universality meaning that any proposed laws are valid regardless of who is considering them, and for what purposes.

On the other hand, all technologies are particular, as they pursue the achievement of specific effects. And for the better part of our technological progress, we can surely state that most technologies achieved their goals with little or no understanding at all, of the natural principles that allowed them to work.

As stated, this situation is viable no more. Our present technology has reached a stage in which trying to produce any new desired effect, skipping for good the part of understanding nature at its most fundamental level, is utterly impossible.

So, any stagnation of our intellectual skills is unlikely to happen to a species capable both of posing deep, fundamental questions—just for the sake of it—and finding their appropriate solutions, as the requirements for technological development are but child's play when compared to the rigor scientific thinking demands.

Thus, if a comet were to theoretically destroy Earth in a couple of thousand of years or earlier, by that time our scientific knowledge would enable us to rapidly develop whatever technological procedures would be deemed as necessary to prevent such a collision. Or, the knowledge might help us move from our Earthly home to whichever other planets or suitable environments in the universe.

# BIBLIOGRAPHY

Darwin, Charles Robert *"The Origin of Species,"* 6th edition. Online, Project Guttenberg Etexts, available for download at http://promo.net/pg/, Jul 31, 2002.

Darwin, Francis (editor) *"The Life and Letters of Charles Darwin."* Online, Project Guttenberg Etexts, available for download at http://promo.net/pg/, Jul 31 2002.

Drexler, K. Eric, *"Engines of Creation,"* Anchor Books, Doubleday, New York, 1986.

Daumas, Maurice, *"Las Grandes Etapas del Progreso Técnico,"* Fondo de Cultura Económica, México, 1983.

Kennedy, Paul, *"The Rise and Fall of the Great Powers—Economic Change and Military Conflict from 1500 to 2000,"* Vintage Books, New York.

Leakey, Richard E., *"The Making of Mankind,"* Abacus Edition, London.

Lorenz, Konrad and others, *"Man and Animal, Studies in Behavior,"* *"Pair-Formation in Ravens,"* St. Martin's Press, New York, 1972.

Malthus, Thomas Robert, *"An Essay on the Principle of Population,"* 1798. Online, Project Guttenberg Etext, available for download at http://promo.net/pg/, Jul 31, 2002.

Pfeiffer, John E., *"The Emergence of Man,"* Third Edition, Harper & Row, Publishers, New York.

Rosenblueth, Arturo, *"El Metodo Científico,"* Consejo Nacional de Ciencia y Tecnología, México, 1981.

Toynbee, Arnold Joseph, *"A Study of History,"* Abridgment of Volumes I-VI by D.C. Somervell, Oxford University Press, New York, Oxford, Reprint Edition 1987.

# NOTES AND REFERENCES

1. Rosenblueth, Arturo, *"El Metodo Científico."*
2. *"World Population Growth from Year 0 to 2050,"* United Nations 1998 Revision, World Population Estimates and Projections, Population Division, Department of Economic and Social Affairs.
3. Press Release POP/656, United Nations, Department of Economic and Social Affairs.
4. Darwin, Francis (editor),*"The Life and Letters of Charles Darwin—Chapter 1.VII.—London and Cambridge—1836-1842."*
5. Ibid 3, Chapter 2, *"Autobiography, My Several Publications."*
6. Malthus, Thomas Robert, *"An Essay on the Principle of Population,"* Chapter 4.
7. Ibid 6, Chapter 4.
8. Darwin, Charles Robert, *"The Origin of Species,"* Chapter I, "VARIATION UNDER DOMESTICATION—PRINCIPLES OF SELECTION ANCIENTLY FOLLOWED, AND THEIR EFFECTS."
9. Ibid 8, Chapter I, "VARIATION UNDER DOMESTICATION—UNCONSCIOUS SELECTION."
10. Milanovic, Branko, *"True world income distribution, 1988 and 1993: First calculation based on household surveys alone,"* October 1999, World Bank, Development Research Group. Online at http://www.worldbank.org/research/transition/abstracts/ineqtrueworld.htm, Nov. 4, 2002. The graph in p. 26 shows nearly 100 million people living in 1993 on $200 dollars a year, which is about 55 cents a day. This income figure was calculated under the Purchasing Power Parity (PPP) method, so that the figure in current US dollars should be smaller.

11. Ibid 8, Chapter II, "DOUBTFUL SPECIES."
12. Toynbee, Arnold J., *"A Study of History,"* Abridgment of Volumes I-VI by Somervell, D.C., p. 35.
13. Daumas, Maurice, *"Las Grandes Etapas del Progreso Técnico"*
14. Pfeiffer, John E., *"The Emergence of Man,"* p. 295. In the same page, the author notes that *"On occasion, controls may break down completely. Murders do occur, along with raids and rare pitched battles involving entire bands."*
15. Ibid 6, Chapter 3.
16. United Nations, *"World Population Prospects: The 2000 Revision,"* Volume III Analytical Report. Online at http://www.un.org/esa/population/publications/wpp2000/wpp2000_volume3.htm, 4 Nov, 2002.
17. Leakey, Richard E., *"The Making of Mankind,"* p. 105.
18. Ibid 6, Chapter 4.
19. Ibid 6, Chapter 3.
20. Ibid 12, p. 4.
21. *"There's Plenty of Room at the Bottom,"* published online at http://www.zyvex.com/nanotech/feynman.html, Nov. 4 2002.
22. U.S. Census Bureau, *"Poverty in the United States: 1998"* (P60-207). Online at http://www.census.gov/hhes/www/povty98.html, Nov 9, 2002.
23. See graphics at Homepage of Hodgson, Dennis, Prof., at http://www.faculty.fairfield.edu/faculty/hodgson/Courses/so11/stratifcation/income&wealth.htm, Nov 9, 2002. The original source of this widely cited data comes from the work of American Economist Dr. Edward Nathan Wolff.
24. Ibid 8, Chapter IV.
25. Lorenz, Konrad, *"Pair-Formation in Ravens."*
26. Ibid 6, Chapter 2.
27. Total Midyear Population for the World: 1950-2050, International Database. Online, at http://www.census.gov/ipc/www/worldpop.html, 4 Nov. 2002
28. Ibid 6, Chapter 4.

# ABOUT THE AUTHOR

Juan J. Gomez-Ibarra was born, raised and educated in Mexico, where he has lived his entire life. Intrigued since a kid by various historical phenomena for which he never found any appropriate answers, he decided to conduct an inquiry on his own, and in the way, he stumbled upon the scientific method. This, his first work, summarizes over twenty years of industry.

0-595-26108-6